SHEPHERDING

a *WOMAN'S* HEART

shepherding

a *woman's* heart

a new model for effective ministry to women

BEVERLY WHITE HISLOP

MOODY PUBLISHERS
CHICAGO

All Scripture quotations, unless otherwise indicated, are taken from the *Holy Bible, New International Version®*. NIV®. Copyright © 1973, 1978, 1984 by International Bible Society. Used by permission of Zondervan Publishing House. All rights reserved.

Scripture quotations marked NASB are taken from the *New American Standard Bible®*, Copyright © The Lockman Foundation 1960, 1962, 1963, 1968, 1971, 1972, 1973, 1975, 1977, 1995. Used by permission.

Scripture quotations marked CEV are taken from the *Contemporary English Version*, Copyright © 1991, 1992, 1995 by American Bible Society. Used by permission.

Scripture quotations marked NLT are taken from the *Holy Bible, New Living Translation*, copyright © 1996. Used by permission of Tyndale House Publishers, Inc., Wheaton Illinois 60189, U.S.A. All rights reserved.

Library of Congress Cataloging-in-Publication Data

Hislop, Beverly White, 1946-
    Shepherding a woman's heart : a new model for effective ministry to women /
Beverly White Hislop.
        p. cm.
    Includes bibliographical references (p.   ).
    ISBN 0-8024-3354-5
    1. Church work with women. 2. Women in church work. I. Title.

BV4445.H57 2003
259'.082--dc21

2003005466

1 3 5 7 9 10 8 6 4 2

Printed in the United States of America

Raymond V. White planted a seed, fertilized, and watered it.
This book is the result. He only had forty-nine years on this earth,
but what a legacy he left.
He modeled godliness, healthy shepherding, and respect for gender differences.
Thanks, Dad, for showing me the way.

James G. Hislop further fertilized and pruned that little oak
by validating my gifting
and the gifting of the many women who have served with us in the body of Christ.
Jim is a leader "above reproach" whose life portrays a Good Shepherd profile
in both church and home.
Thanks, honey, for opening the way.

contents

section one
develop an awareness
reasons we need it

section two
deepen understanding
reasons to give it

section three
disperse compassion
people who need it

section four
diversify skills
people who give it

acknowledgments

the warmth and expertise of the team at Moody Publishers have increased the joy of this journey immensely! Communicating with you has been reminiscent of my first piano recital. I was both surprised and gratified that people came and that they applauded the performance of my first piece. The greatest amazement was that my piano teacher who had so graciously and relentlessly coached me to the place of readiness to "go public" did not have her name next to mine in the program. I want to make sure the names of the strong Moody team are on this program! Thank you Elsa Mazon, Anne Scherich, Pam Pugh, and Amy Peterson!

There are many who have indirectly contributed to this book through their input in my life. I am grateful for the teams of women who graciously embraced me and the seedbed of ideas sprouted in this book. I so value the journey we shared in developing and expanding ministries to women in churches in Germany, Orlando, Portland, North Palm Beach, and Gresham.

GRACE COMMUNITY CHURCH

I appreciate the first team of women at Grace Community Church who were willing to take a risk and be part of an evolutionary process of developing a pastoral care to women approach to ministry to women: Arlys Bucher, Beth Cunningham, Kathy Crannell, Shirley Hadley, Tamara Russell, and Alma Lou Tischler.

The tears of joy streaming down my face as I drove home from that first "rebuilding team" meeting were evidence that my passion for ministry to women in the local church was stronger than ever. It felt like an essential part of who God made me to be had been rediscovered. Thank you, Shirley, for loving me and opening the door for me to love and be loved by the awesome women at GCC! Thanks to subsequent teams, especially Beth Cunningham and Kathy Crannell, who have continued to include me in their lives and ministry development. You have taught me so much! Thanks to Pastors Dennis and Jim and the elders for their incredible ability to shepherd well.

WESTERN SEMINARY:

The support and encouragement from President Bert Downs and Dr. Randy Roberts have been assuring and energizing. To the faculty and staff: Thank you for creating a diet and climate that fosters a ministry of training, resources, and networking for women in ministry like the Women's Center for Ministry. The heart of the Good Shepherd is seen daily in you, Kenine. I count it a privilege to serve alongside you. What a joy it has been to minister with such colleagues of sterling character and "can do" attitudes. Our students also remind me that no investment is too great when God is in it!

FAMILY:

I am grateful for my mother, Connie Stiles, who as a young woman called out to a God whom she did not know personally. God certainly met you and has shown Himself to you through all these years, especially through the deaths of two husbands. Your journey is an incredible testimony of God's unconditional love and grace. Thank you, Mom, for staying on your knees on behalf of me and my three siblings, Paul, P. D., and Carole and our families.

Thank you, my own precious daughter, Lorraine, for understanding that a call to ministry is a sacrifice that impacts family. Dan, your creativity still ignites my own. Lorraine and Gene, Dan and Maureen you are God's greatest gifts to us and we are indeed blessed. Thank you for six precious grandchildren, who we imagine will grow up to delight and challenge your hearts, as you did ours: Madeline, Katie, Emma, Hannah, Zachary, and Matthew. And to my incredible husband, Jim, I dedicate this book.

preface: a special message for pastors and church leaders

I have been married to a pastor for thirty-five years and have served as director of women's ministries for many of those years. I understand many of the challenges of the pastoral role. People with the best of intentions often bring new ideas and new resources for the pastor to read and consider. There is little time to read all of the resources and even less time to try to implement them.

This is not a call for pastors to do more. Rather it is a call to further multiply the good work you are already doing by infusing the women in your church with the same spirit that moves you to offer pastoral care to your flock. More than 50 percent (some statistics show 75 percent) of the people in your congregation are women. Imagine how your own shepherding load could be lightened if healthy women were available to come alongside hurting women for encouragement and support! Not only could this advance your ministry goals, it could encourage women to fulfill scriptural injunctions by offering help and hope to other women. In this way ministry would be multiplied.

Men are an essential part of a woman's life, as evidenced in God's original plan for men and women. A male perspective is critical for balance and health. A female perspective is also needed for balance and health. The Titus 2 directive clearly incorporates both. Psychological and physiological evidence supports the biblical description of male and female differences. Given the clear message that healthy women focus on relationships as nurturers, does it not seem biblical and logical that women would be the best candidates for shepherding women in emotional pain?

One of the nine reasons given in chapter 2 for women shepherding women is to reduce the risk of emotional or physical adultery between male pastors and women parishioners. Understanding that a woman in emotional pain is particularly vulnerable is another good reason for women to shepherd women.

Add to this the fact that some women are unable to receive pastoral care from men, due to the source of past pain. Who will shepherd these women to health if not another woman?

Pastor, I invite you to review the table of contents and selectively read chapters that focus on questions that remain. Would you then consider giving "trustworthy" women in your church the freedom to begin developing Shepherds of Women? Encourage these women to read this book with a serious heart:

1. Pray while reading this book, asking God to make clear His will for *your* church.

2. Discuss the book together, then brainstorm options.

3. Share ideas on how to begin assessing the needs in your church: modify and distribute the sample survey, compile results, and talk to women about their needs.

4. Cast the vision for shepherding women. Use the inspirational material in this book as a resource to lay the foundation.

5. Build a team, bringing together women who have experienced emotional pain but are healed and understand the issues causing pain. Bring together women who are godly and trustworthy (Titus 2). Build team cohesion while exploring training options.

6. Mold the ministry around the need profile (see chapter 10).

Women in pain are in every congregation. These women often feel misunderstood and even marginalized. Too many times this drives women out of the church and into places of further victimization and pain. Does not the example of the good shepherd in John 10 and of the good shepherding of Ezekiel 34 implore us to provide care for these members of the body of Christ? What better way to offer healing and grace than to have women available who understand like-pain and can offer pastoral care?

In the midst of the decadent society of Crete, Paul's injunction to penetrate that society focused on developing church leadership and teaching older men, older women, and younger men, with one people group obviously missing. The *younger women* were to be trained by the older godly women. Paul's message is clear. Godly character in relationship could have a powerful impact on a decadent society such as Crete, or your city! The relationship between women is a critical aspect of impacting our culture.

Pastor, I appeal to the God-given responsibility that you take so seriously for the welfare of the women in your church to become godly, healthy, reproducing disciples. As your leadership provides the climate and diet needed for older women to grow in godliness, would you then encourage these older women to take the initiative to then train younger women? To consider ways of shepherding women?

Then the healthy, the young, the lost, and the injured women in your church community may all begin to look more like the godly women of Titus 2.

BEV HISLOP

develop an awareness

reasons we need it

the focus of shepherding women

I sat across the lunch table from a former key staff member of a well-known Christian ministry. We briefly exchanged stories and then Carol (not her real name) said, "Bev, tell me the truth. Do you see any hope in the church?"

"Hope?" I asked.

Carol continued.

> After my husband, a committed church leader, walked out on our twenty-year marriage for a younger woman, I was devastated. I wish I could tell you someone from the church expressed care, understanding, or support. But instead, everyone avoided me—no one called or even came to pray with me.
>
> After meeting with our pastor, I realized that even he did not understand how much pain I was in. All he said was to make sure I studied the Bible and prayed every day.

Frankly, I wish I could have studied the Bible every day, but the pain and shock of it all hurt so deeply there were days I thought I wouldn't be able to catch my next breath, let alone concentrate enough to read or study. I could only pray three words, "Help me, Jesus!"

The most humiliating day of my life was the day I finally walked into my doctor's office to ask for an AIDS test. Even though I had remained pure before and during my marriage, when I found my husband was a sex addict, I knew I was at risk. It took me weeks to gather the courage to go. As I approached the receptionist, I looked around, felt my face grow hot, then whispered, "I came for an AIDS test." I felt so alone and so ashamed.

Bev, do you ever see the church becoming a place where people understand pain like this and express care to people in my situation?

Frankly, I rarely go to church any more. The pain is too great.

Is this a unique story? I wish it were.

Usually I am a defender of the church. I believe it is Christ's bride, His body on earth. Having been a pastor's wife for many years, I know it is more difficult to bring about change on the inside than it appears to be from the outside. It is also easier to criticize what the church is not doing than it is to jump in and contribute to the solution.

But on that winter day in February, I heard Carol's pain. I had heard it too many times before. And I had no words of defense to offer.

Each school term I hear students of all ages express similar pain. Women often tell me that my seminary classroom is the first place they have found where they could admit their source of pain and feel accepted and understood.

I have discovered that once students hear the story of a woman who has experienced the pain of abortion, divorce, or domestic violence they begin to feel a new level of compassion. Once students feel compassion, they open their hearts for an increased awareness of the issue causing the pain. This deeper understanding of the pain motivates students to acquire shepherding skills. This progression has become predictable.

Often in our desire to resist sin, we can miss seeing a real person behind a past sin. Even when we know domestic violence is wrong, we can transfer our doubts about the "real story" behind the scenes onto the victim. Then we find it hard to feel compassion or express care. We are still in the judging stage, wondering if she "deserves" our intervention. The very ones she had hoped would understand and offer care only multiply the enormous pain and self-doubt she already feels. She is again marginalized and further immobilized.

We look at our full slate of Bible studies and women's ministry programs and wonder why women like Carol do not feel accepted or why they are not involved. Our beautifully decorated Christmas Luncheons and Spring Teas are not pulling her in. Our busy pastors may meet with her. She may even attend Sunday services. But we sense that we are not really connecting with her. We are not really meeting her where she is. What do we do for her? Where does she fit?

Just as a paramedic first looks at the source of the bleeding, we should focus first on the injury. A patient who is bleeding profusely cannot receive instruction on how the accident might have been prevented. What the patient needs at that point is emergency care from someone who understands what is needed to stop the bleeding and what are the "normal" symptoms of his specific injury. Once the initial source of bleeding is discovered and addressed, then more long-term and even preventive instruction can be received from the patient's established health care provider.

Too often the body of Christ starts with preventive instruction, then long-term directives. The woman is told to memorize Scripture or pray more. This is valuable and needful instruction, but it is not timely when the patient is bleeding emotionally, panic-stricken, or confused. In essence, women are often told, "Just get over it! Stop the tears and just move on. This isn't that bad."

effective pastoral care to women reverses the usual order of procedure

My friend Carol needed someone to be present with her in her pain. She needed someone who could encourage her to cry even when she was afraid she might not stop crying. She needed someone who understood that feelings of shock, disbelief, anger, and bargaining are all part of the grief process. She needed someone safe encouraging her to express her feelings of betrayal and injustice.

It *is* healthy to feel the pain. Crying is cathartic. It is an essential step toward healing.

Once the patient is given emotional CPR, she is watched carefully for stabilizing responses and treated accordingly. Our first concern in giving directive instructions should be her emotional state. Once she is in a safe place and stabilized emotionally, she can think more clearly.

Effective pastoral care to women focuses first on the emotional pain and how women process emotional pain. Then it gives attention to the issues that cause women pain. A shepherd would know that Carol needed to feel the pain before she was ready to think about the next step of her life. A shepherd responds with compassion. She skillfully dispenses pastoral care that is timely and appropriate. Finally, effective pastoral care continues to move toward the goal of bringing this woman to a place of health. The caregiver understands that this will take time and multiple resources. She coaches the woman toward making decisions that lead to health and maturity. A shepherd knows when to refer to professionals while offering the pastoral care needed on the journey to recovery.

a shepherd of women will stop the bleeding before she gives the vitamins

"Bev, do you ever see the church becoming a place where people understand pain like this and express care to people in my situation?"

Yes, yes, yes, Carol. I *do* see hope in the church! I too dream of the church's becoming a place where people understand pain like yours and express care to people in your situation. Certainly a new focus, a new model of ministering to women is needed.

One such model identifies women who are available to come alongside women in pain. These potential Shepherds of Women have

- experienced emotional pain,
- received healing,
- gained understanding of the issue(s) causing them pain,
- received training,
- modeled the four Titus 2 characteristics, and
- been approved by the pastoral staff.

A resource list is compiled of women willing to be identified as Shepherds of Women to come alongside women in pain. Pastoral staff and other church leaders then use this list as the need arises.

A new model of women's ministry focuses on Shepherds of Women as central to providing truly *effective* ministry to the broad scope of the needs of women. The focus is on the women themselves, more than on popular programs or events. Bible studies and events certainly are part of the model but only as their purpose clearly ministers to a defined people group. The purpose in ministering to each people group is unequivocally to lead women to the Living Water, Jesus Christ. But some women can only receive sips of water from a teaspoon. In our eagerness to quench thirsts, we sometimes use a fire hose.

This book is written in the hope that we can contribute to the solution rather than to criticize what the church is not doing. *We* are the church, Christ's body.

Carol, as a member of Christ's body, I apologize to you and the many women like you who have experienced incredible pain, marginalization, and loss from the church because we have not reached out to you in your pain with understanding and compassion. I am so sorry! May you find it in your heart to forgive us. I know the Good Shepherd would wish more for His body. Oh, forgive us, Lord! Show us a new way. Show us the way of a shepherd.

Men and women, I invite you to explore with me the elements needed to shift our focus so that we can begin to change this tide, one woman at a time. Perhaps the next Carol who comes through our church door will feel the awareness, understanding, compassion, and skillful shepherding that Jesus would have given. Then this book will have served its purpose.

the need for shepherds of women

CASANDRA RETURNED HOME from college to work on some personal issues. She was a very capable, friendly young woman who knew the Lord personally and had attended church for several years. Casandra admitted that all her life she had been working to become the boy her dad so wanted but did not have. That desire led her into sinful actions, and she now had a strong desire to change her lifestyle.

Casandra's counselor pointed out that she lacked a sense of what it meant to be a woman "on the inside." Casandra needed to spend time with a "feminine" woman to discover the essence of her own gender. I agreed to meet regularly with Casandra to restructure the foundation of her own gender. During those months, Casandra continued to see her counselor to work through some deeper issues. Each week Casandra would talk with me about her discoveries and struggles. She worked hard to process what her counselor led her to discover, integrating it into the gender foundation she was building.

Casandra's story increases our awareness of the need for women to shepherd women. First we will look at nine reasons women are the best candidates to shepherd women. Then we will look at how shepherding and counseling work together.

WHY WOMEN ARE THE BEST CANDIDATES TO SHEPHERD WOMEN

1. Women best model godly femininity.

Casandra needed a woman to help her sort out the gender messages in her life. This need is increasing in a culture that often blurs the lines or demands gender rights or superiority. Although a man may be able to clearly *define* femininity, who could better *model* godly gender characteristics of a woman than a woman? Women need to know what godliness looks like in a feminine body. Similarly, Scripture gives a paint-by-number picture of a godly woman in texts such as Titus 2. But women in each culture, time zone, and family system must fill in the color. "Women are mirrors for our femaleness our whole life long. . . . Women always need other women to come alongside and speak their language: the language of the heart and of feelings. We shape each other's attitudes and self-definitions as we converse and from each other we learn what it means to be female."[1]

Feminine perspective balances the masculine perspective that is most often heard in our public church services or from our fathers. Feminine perspective enables a woman to apply biblical passages strategically. Women shepherds reflect that perspective in "the language of the heart and of feelings," in a medium that is best understood and translated in the particulars of a woman's daily life. She models godly femininity.

2. Generally, women process pain differently from men.

Women seem to have a greater need to talk through their experience, to feel the emotions of the experience again as they talk.

They need to tell their story—get it all out—before they can begin to take steps toward healing. Often men want 1-2-3 steps to healing without desiring to re-experience the pain through "telling." Men usually put their feelings on hold until they put their thoughts on the table. This is often the reason many women feel a lack of healing after hearing a male church leader's advice to read the Bible more, or pray more, or "try harder to love him." The most important step for women has been bypassed.[2]

A study by Broverman and her associates examined traits characteristically associated with masculinity and femininity. A group of practicing therapists was asked to identify characteristics that best described a healthy adult man, a healthy adult woman, and a healthy adult. The lists of characteristics for the healthy adult male and healthy adult were closely aligned. However, the correlation was lower between the healthy adult woman and the healthy adult. If a woman earned a high rating as a healthy woman, she could not simultaneously earn a high rating as a healthy adult. If she earned a high rating as a healthy adult, she could not also receive a high rating as a healthy woman. She could not be both a healthy adult and a healthy woman. Some used this study to validate the idea that the standard of mental health was masculine in nature. Counselors were led to counsel women toward a healthy male model and away from a healthy female model.[3]

Often we can find this same tendency in pastoral care. Instead, women should be cared for within the framework of a healthy *adult female* profile. Certainly one important aspect of this framework is understanding that women process pain differently than men.

3. Women understand women.

Much of the emotional pain women experience is related to being created as life-bearers and life-nurturers. The physiological seasons of a woman's life, along with her many relational and professional roles in life, generate painful issues. "There are times when being a woman just plain hurts. At any age from puberty to menopause, menses can be the source of extreme discomfort."[4] Of the 42 million women in this country who suffer from these symptoms, some "3.5 million have symptoms so severe that they are unable to function for one to two days each month. . . . When estrogen and progesterone levels drop, so do . . . drive, ambition and mood."[5] These hormonal variants are best understood by women.

And who can better relate to the emotional and physical impact of abortion, PMS, childbirth, or menopause than a woman? "We are different [from men] anatomically, hormonally, socially, sexually, psychologically and emotionally."[6] Peter acknowledged this difference when he instructed husbands to "treat [your wives] with respect as the weaker partners" (1 Peter 3:7). A woman's monthly cycle, childbearing season, and, later, menopause bring a biologically "weaker" aspect to a woman's life. A woman feels emotionally weaker during times of hormonal changes. These clearly impact and even create emotional pain best understood by a woman. When a woman feels understood, she is more likely to share her pain and thus begin a journey of healing.

4. Most women have natural shepherding abilities as nurturers.

Many of the skills needed to shepherd women are essentially nurturing skills. "Women proceed from a different frame of reference than men. They work first from a position of concerned involvement and caring. . . . Their frame of reference includes sensitivity unique to them . . . and includes deepened empathy [the ability to comprehend another's experience]. . . . Girls and women focus on care."[7]

As God's choice life-bearers, women have been given the inherent skills needed to bring a person from babyhood to adulthood emotionally, mentally, spiritually, and physically. These skills are transferable to shepherding a woman from a place of emotional and spiritual pain and illness to a place of health. Even women who have diminished nurturing skills because of painful pasts find something within that responds to re-parenting or training. "A woman . . . tends to value giving something of herself to nourish relationships and deepen attachments. Her focus is . . . more on *entering a relational* network . . . *involvement* and *attachment* and *invitation* belong more clearly to feminine identity."[8] Certainly these abilities are essential for effective shepherding.

5. Women shepherding women may reduce the risk of emotional or physical adultery between male pastors and women parishioners.

The statistics on this malady in our churches continue to escalate. Many times the beginnings of an unhealthy relationship occur when women are emotionally vulnerable. "Particularly in situations of sexual abuse, for example, the problem in pastoral response is not too little empathy but too much indiscriminate empathy by an uninformed pastoral caregiver that surfaces long-repressed feelings that overwhelm rather than help the person in need."[9]

A woman experiencing emotional trauma or pain is a woman who is emotionally vulnerable. A woman in pain may wrongly interpret words and touch intended to offer solace. Her past grid may influence her to interpret expressions of tenderness by a male as a sexual advance. Ruth Senter concludes: "Male associations are more likely to be safe territory for us if we feel content with our own husband. The minute I begin to feel my husband is not enough for me, I set myself up for inappropriate involvement with someone else."[10]

A kind shepherding response is often like a cold drink of water in a desert or a tantalizing feast at a time of extreme emotional famine. A healthy woman shepherd may divert this potential temptation to impropriety with a man.

Certainly, precautions need to be taken in any relationship, and relationships between women are no exception. Healthy boundaries and accountability contribute to healthy relationships between women. Women shepherds need to be sensitive and alert to sexual issues with their own gender as well as with men. All relationships should be handled with understanding and caution.

6. Some women are unable to receive shepherding from men.

Unfortunately, some of the pain women have experienced in the past and experience in the present has been perpetrated by men—

uncles, fathers, brothers, husbands, coworkers. In the same way that medication enables a patient to be relaxed before receiving the benefit of a cleansed and repaired wound, so a woman's soul must be open to a caregiver's offering of cleansing and repair to her emotional wounds. This is nearly impossible in the presence of fear or resistance, the emotions most often felt by many women who have been wounded by men.

7. Women shepherding women will enhance effectiveness of limited pastoral staff resources.

Most church staffs are stretched to the limit with myriad church concerns. It is nearly impossible to give each parishioner the kind of one-to-one care that is desired. Having a resource list of women shepherds who are available to come alongside women in difficulties could literally be a life-saving asset to a church body.

8. Women are given spiritual gifts needed for shepherding.

Spiritual gifts are not gender specific. All the gifts are given to both men and women. The lists of recipients in the primary biblical passages on spiritual gifts (Romans 12; 1 Corinthians 12; Ephesians 4; 1 Peter 4) are clearly not differentiated as to men and women. "Nowhere are gifts classified according to sexes," some allotted to men and others to women.[11] The New Testament places no limit on what gifts a woman may or may not have (the word *pastor* is used in a list of spiritual gifts in Ephesians 4, not as a church office). Women are certainly given gifts needed for effective shepherding.

9. It is biblical!

If the text in Titus 2 says anything to the church, it instructs women to shepherd women. Looking at the context of Paul's message to Titus may give a new perspective on this time-honored passage. Before we look at this aspect in more detail (see chapter 3), let's consider the relationship between counseling and shepherding.

how shepherding and
counseling work together

Casandra's story illustrates the need for both shepherding and professional counseling. Can they co-exist? What does counseling offer? What does shepherding offer? What is a shepherd of women? Is it the same as extending pastoral care to women? How is being a shepherd to women different from counseling or spiritual direction?

In some ways, pastoral care to women includes elements of mentoring, pastoral counseling, spiritual direction, and discipleship. These comprise the components of shepherding. So pastoral care and shepherding essentially are synonymous.

The agenda for one-to-one shepherding is generally determined by the woman in need and may include many aspects of the process identified for other caring roles. The caregiver may be called upon to facilitate, coach, listen, pray, or transmit information. This relationship may even develop to a level of mentor or disciple.

The greatest distinction of a shepherd is that she is a woman who intentionally provides the comfort and understanding that fosters healing and growth.

A pastoral caregiver to women expresses understanding out of a heart of compassion. She facilitates the process the wounded woman will walk through toward healing. She gently listens and asks questions that help the woman process her pain, reveals options the woman can chose, and respects the woman's own ability to make choices. She prays with and for the woman. When it is appropriate, she will give biblical comfort and provide a biblical perspective on the issue causing pain. Her role is to put the wounded woman's hand into the hand of the Good Shepherd. This may at first involve being His hands and feet. It may involve playing the music of the gospel of Christ before saying the words. But the ultimate desire is to see the woman become a healthy, reproducing disciple of Jesus Christ. Shepherds will minister to the healthy as well as the wounded.

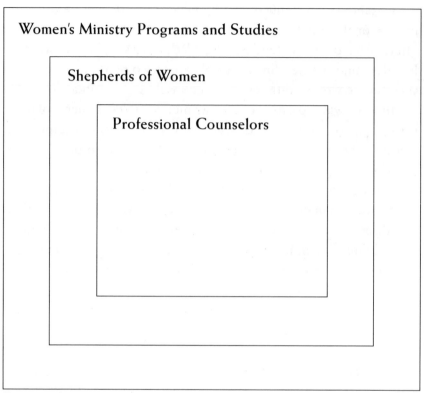

Fig. 2.1.

Traditionally, Women's Ministries are planned programs for women in the church. These include events, women's Bible studies, moms' groups, and prayer groups. Shepherding, by contrast, is generally given one-to-one, although small group pastoral care is viable. Professional counseling, on the other hand, is called for when more long-standing and involved issues arise. Counselors may be able to better answer the "Why am I behaving this way?" questions. Understanding the *why* often frees a client to make choices to change behavior or lifestyles. So professional counseling is often a sub-component of an overall ministry to women (see Fig. 2.1).

Professional counseling is called for when more long-standing and involved issues arise. How do professional counseling and shepherding interface? Here are some of the components of professional counseling.

1. *Professional counseling focuses on pathologies.* The client wants to know "What is wrong with me?" The need for change is implied. Diagnosis involves determining what is unhealthy about the individual. It identifies a negative factor.

2. *Professional counseling is a one-way relationship.* Developing a mutual friendship with a client could obscure the counselor's objectivity, making appropriate confrontation less likely and potentially limit sharing by the client lest the friendship be compromised. The counselor will not intentionally share her feelings, her story, or her life with her client. It is a professional relationship.

3. *Professional counseling contact time is very costly and therefore limited.* It will likely be no more than one hour weekly. Most professional counseling is conducted in an office. This contact is to be kept strictly confidential unless there is a signed release, threat of harm to self or others, or a court order mandating an exception.

4. *The professional counselor is trained to be strong emotionally, to monitor her own affect with clients.* She is not to express personal feelings. She hopefully will be empathetic—to verbally communicate understanding of the client's feelings—but will not sympathize, nor will she share the client's feelings or feel them with the client. To do so would inhibit her ability to direct the client amidst the client's emotional instability. She is trained to counsel in a professional manner.

5. *Professional counselors study human development, psychopathology, assessment, statistics, research, and legal and ethical issues, in addition to counseling techniques.* Past patterns of human behavior give insight into present pathologies.

6. *Professional counselors are not always free to integrate prayer or Bible study into the counseling session.* Due to insurance requirements, often clients must go to secular counselors, who are clearly not free to overtly discuss biblical truths. The counselor is free, however, to walk a client through a client's own belief system in the process of counseling. Some larger churches may have professional counselors on staff or a list of established referrals who have the benefit of integrating a spiritual dynamic into their counseling sessions.[12]

Professional counseling is beneficial for many hurting women. However, *most of the long-term healing work takes place outside of the counseling office.* Once the client makes a choice to change behavior or lifestyle, the hard work of implementing begins. This is when women especially need someone to walk alongside them. So women need shepherding while they are going to a professional counselor. A woman needs someone to listen and help her process her discoveries once she leaves the counseling office. She needs someone from whom she can receive care, acceptance, and sympathy in the midst of her emotional pain.

Casandra's counselor certainly gave her an understanding of how past patterns of human behavior give insight into present pathologies. This information was essential in her journey. But it was the consistent time with a shepherd that helped her process the pain while supplying one brick at a time to lay a new foundation. It was her shepherd who received phone calls late at night when Casandra was in the middle of an internal struggle that required immediate prayer and accountability. It was the shepherd who gave Casandra an appropriate scriptural truth to memorize to strengthen her mind and heart. It was her shepherd who spent time with Casandra modeling femininity. A woman shepherd was critical for Casandra's journey toward healing.

Not only is this kind of shepherding to women a good idea, it is biblical. Our next chapter will focus on the biblical basis for women shepherding women.

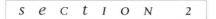
d e e p e n
UNDERSTANDING

reasons to give it

eternaL understandinG: bibLicaL basis

katrina had just finished her first year of college. One of her courses led to class discussions on femininity and masculinity. The class concluded that there was no real difference in the genders, only the impact of socialization. The clear implication was that society should not make any gender distinctions in places such as public restrooms, clothing store departments, or medical offices. Society was unjust in treating children or adults differently because of gender. If a given culture would treat its youth without bias, men and women would become very similar in outward appearance, work preferences, and even personality. People would then be truly free to become themselves.

Katrina came home wondering, *Is there any innate difference between men and women, masculinity and femininity? If a woman doesn't like makeup, lace, fingernail polish, or skirts, does that mean she isn't feminine? If a man enjoys a nursing career, does that mean he isn't masculine? Is nurture the answer* to the long-debated nature versus nurture question? Does the Bible reveal a clear difference?

The Bible certainly encourages woman to intentionally match outward appearance with inward core values (1 Timothy 2:9–10; 1 Peter 3:3–4), and Scripture gives room for men to pursue helping professions (1 Corinthians 10:24; Galatians 6:10; Colossians 3:23–24). But does the Bible give a clear description of what is the essential core of a woman, as opposed to a man? Is there a difference in the sexes in this essential core? If so, how will that difference be reflected in a woman's life? And how will the answer impact *our* ability to shepherd a woman's heart? To find an answer, let's look at the beginning.

the essential beginning of woman

Man and woman had similar beginnings.

> *So God created man in his own image,*
> *In the image of God he created him;*
> *Male and female he created them.*

> *God blessed them and said to them, "Be fruitful and increase in number, fill the earth and subdue it. Rule over the fish of the sea and the birds of the air and over every living creature that moves on the ground." (Genesis 1:27–28)*

Since there were probably no dishes to wash, no clothes to launder, no house to vacuum, no groceries to buy, and no chauffeuring needed, God's original intent for the woman must have been broader than those services. We observe, instead, that both male and female were created in God's image, with shared tasks of ruling over creation and reproducing. God communicated those tasks to both the man and the woman in the same hearing. Both needed each other to accomplish God's grand purposes for them on earth. God blessed them, "male and female."

Yet in Genesis 2 we begin seeing differences between the man's and the woman's early experiences. We observe three things true about Adam that were not true about Eve.

1. *Adam was formed from dust.* "The LORD God formed the man from the dust of the ground. . . . Now the LORD God had formed out of the ground all the beasts [and] birds" (Genesis 2:7, 19). The cohabitants of man's world were the animals, also formed from the dust of the ground. His first experiences were with the animals and the plants of the garden.

2. *Adam received his initial job description directly from God.* "The LORD God took the man and put him in the Garden of Eden to work it and take care of it. And the LORD God commanded the man, 'You are free to eat from any tree in the garden, but you must not eat from the tree of the knowledge of good and evil.' . . . Whatever the man called each living creature, that was its name" (Genesis 2:15–16, 19).

   Adam was to (a) name the animals, (b) work the garden, (c) maintain the garden, and (d) eat from any tree but one. Life for Adam consisted of achievement, of completing tasks without the help or companionship of another human being. From the beginning, man focused on "work," on "tasks" given to him by God Himself.

3. *Adam was incomplete without a suitable helper.* Adam's world consisted of plants, animals, food, God, and life purpose in a perfect environment. What more could he need? Yet, "the LORD God said, 'It is not good for the man to be alone'" (Genesis 2:18). Man lacked companionship with his own kind. Even the animals had this. For Adam, "no suitable helper was found" (v. 20). God saw human companionship as the essential piece needed to make man complete. *God's intention was for man to complete his tasks in relationship.* Thus man, who was so capable of the tasks God had previously given, was now given a woman to enable him to do this—and his

job description was modified: embrace his wife and rule relationally. Man would be completed by woman as a result of his drawing her to himself.[1]

Four things were true about Eve that were not true about Adam.

1. *Woman was formed from a man's rib, establishing relationship.* "The LORD God caused the man to fall into a deep sleep; and while he was sleeping, he took one of the man's ribs and closed up the place with flesh. Then the LORD God made a woman from the rib he had taken out of the man, and he brought her to the man" (Genesis 2:21–22). It is unclear how God manifested His presence before sin, but we do know that Adam and Eve "heard the sound of the LORD God as he was walking in the garden in the cool of the day" (3:8). It is likely that the first Being both Adam and Eve sensed after their first breath was God.

   Eve's second encounter was with another human being, Adam. Since Adam was asleep during the rib transplant (one wonders if the Surgeon explained post-operatively that Adam was the donor!), Eve was the first and only human to be formed in this unique way from another human being. Unlike Adam, the origin of her body came directly from another human, imaging relationship.

2. *Woman began life in community.* Eve received community living instructions from Adam. Adam must have communicated to Eve his job description: take care of the garden, eat from any plant *but one*, and so on. We don't know how Adam communicated God's mandate about not eating the fruit of that one tree in the garden, but we assume Eve received this life-altering instruction secondhand from Adam. Eve began life in community.

3. *Woman was complete from the beginning.* Unlike Adam, Eve was never without companionship. God had created a per-

fect environment, complete with animals, plants, food, life purpose, and a companion—to say nothing of the presence of God Himself! God had provided all she needed to be complete, to be fulfilled.

4. *Woman completed God's initial creation.* It was "not good for the man to be alone" (Genesis 2:18), but God concluded it was "very good" when the woman was created (1:31). During the seven days of creation, only once did God describe His creative works in the superlative and that was after He created woman. She completed His great work of creation. She was the "finishing touch"!

So from the beginning there were two core differences:

From the beginning, Adam's first experiences were without human companions.
Adam focused on his work, on the tasks before him.
From the beginning, Eve's first experiences were in human relationship.

INSiGHtS fRom tHE faLL

Genesis 3 provides further insight into the lives of the first man and woman. Even though we know the curse is descriptive—not prescriptive—we can learn something from its focus.

• For the woman, the impact of the Fall was primarily felt in her *relationships.* "I will greatly increase your pains in childbearing; with pain you will give birth to children. Your desire will be for your husband, and he will rule over you" (Genesis 3:16).

• For the man, the impact of the Fall was primarily experienced in his *tasks and work.* "Cursed is the ground because of you; through painful toil you will eat of it all the days of your life. It will produce thorns and thistles for you, and you will eat the plants of the field. By the sweat of your brow you will eat your food until you return to the ground, since from it you were taken; for dust you are and to dust you will return" (Genesis 3:17–19).

A closer look at the focus of the curse clearly reveals a twofold impact for the woman: (1) her relationship with her children and (2) her relationship with her husband. These are obviously a married mother's primary relationships. Does this have meaning for single women? Does this reflect the nature of a woman? What is the essential nature of a woman?

tHe essentiaL natuRe of woman

Distilling the nature of a woman to the essential elements is indeed a challenge. As we lay the biblical foundation for shepherding women, we begin with two essential elements listed in Scripture: woman as life-bearer and woman as companion.

Woman as Life-Bearer

Genesis 5:2 intimates that both man and woman were called *Adam,* or *man* (woman "coming out of man") when they were created. Yet the first words in the text after the curse (Genesis 3:14–19) were Adam's, and in these words Adam, the namer, draws a key distinction between himself and his wife. He clearly differentiates between himself and her by giving the woman her own name, *Eve,* one that means *living,* "because she would become the mother of all the living" (Genesis 3:20).

After hearing the curse given to the serpent—"Cursed are you above all the livestock and all the wild animals! You will crawl on your belly and you will eat dust all the days of your life"—Adam also heard God's message that the reversal of his and Eve's sin would come through the woman's offspring. The serpent's head would be crushed—and Eve would mother that offspring (vv. 14–15).

In the next chapter we witness "the mother of all the living" giving birth to their first child. It was during the painful birth process that Eve acknowledged, perhaps for the first time since the Fall, her need for the Lord's help: "With the help of the LORD I have brought forth a man" (4:1).

Does bearing children solely define a woman? What about single women or married women without children? Is childbearing simply a physical, biological difference between men and women? Or has God so created woman so that *every fiber* of her being is made to nurture others? Would it not be consistent with God's character to create a human being with the ability to gestate with all the *emotional, mental,* and *spiritual capabilities* that are needed to take care of that life and to prepare that little one for interdependent living?

Life experiences can damage or hinder the full development of this nurturing capacity, but the Creator designed women with nurturing abilities as standard equipment. Married or single—women who bear biological children and women who don't—are all created with a nurturing bent.

Since the development of anesthetics, the physical pain of childbirth is diminished, though not excluded completely, for most women. Giving birth is still physically painful. But giving birth involves much more than carrying a child in the womb for nine months and then pushing that child through the birth canal. Women who, for various reasons, do not keep the infant they have carried in the womb can still experience incredible emotional and mental trauma. Does not life-experience bear out what we instinctively know? God has intentionally designed the life-bearer with life-nurturing qualities —qualities that when further developed will cultivate a new life from inter-uterine stages to birth to interdependent adulthood.

Does this mean that my body defines who I am? Jesus responded to the woman who cried out, "Blessed is the mother who gave you birth and nursed you," with the bigger picture of life purpose: "Blessed rather are those who hear the word of God and obey it" (Luke 11:27–28). Jesus was saying that the greatest thing about a woman is not her womb or her breasts—her body—but rather hearing and obeying God. Our Creator gave us a spirit with which we can know and reflect God. The body He gives each human being is a body consistent with His plan for that life. A woman's spirit would naturally be "clothed" in a feminine body. The nurturing nature the Creator gave women fits beautifully with the spirit and body, enabling women to encourage others, to bring health and beauty to relationships on earth.

Woman as Companion

The second relationship impacted by the Fall was the marriage relationship. The woman was told, "Your desire will be for your husband, and he will rule over you" (Genesis 3:16).

Yes, in the same way that motherhood would be difficult, so the marriage relationship would have its challenges. As a matter of fact, *all* relationships would feel the impact of sin. The most intimate of God-designed relationships is one where the man and the woman are "one flesh." Intimacy on every level is intimated in those words.

Woman would have a continual "desire" for her husband. The Hebrew word *teshukah*, translated "desire" here, is used in Scripture only two other times.[2] The most common comparison is made to Genesis 4:7, where the Lord says to Cain, "Sin is crouching at your door; it *desires* to have you, but you must master it" (italics added). Often the assumption is made that woman's desire is sinful; it is a desire to rule over her husband and she must master it. However, the Hebrew word *teshukah* does not convey that idea. Rather, the context of Genesis 4:7 suggests *control*. Some would see the need to interpret all of Genesis 3:16 as a negative, since it is given in the context of the curse. Yet, certainly no one would frame birthing children (v. 16) or eating plants for food (v. 18) as intrinsically "bad" things. It is the impact of the curse that has made these good things difficult or even painful.

A comparison made with a Scripture in a similar context, the marriage relationship, will shed more light on our interpretation. The only other time the Hebrew word *teshukah* is used in the Bible is in the Song of Songs: "I belong to my lover, and his *desire* is for me" (7:10; italics added). The word means longing, attraction, runs after. The bridegroom longs for his bride! She, in turn, wants him to desire her in the same way she desires him. Verses 11 and 12 reflect a beautiful longing for intimacy with her groom: "Come, my lover, let us go to the countryside, let us spend the night in the villages. . . . There I will give you my love."

A healthy wife will *desire* intimacy with her husband. Wives whose husbands do not respond lovingly to their overtures of love still *longingly desire* an intimate relationship with their spouses! Even domestic violence victims often *want* to return to a love relationship with their husbands.

This desire for intimacy is so strong in women that often they believe that true happiness and fulfillment can only be found in a relationship with a man. Often Christian women erroneously expect a husband to meet all of their needs for intimacy, when only Christ can fill the deepest longings of our soul. God made women with a need for intimacy. Women have a strong desire to meet this need in relationship. Could this desire for a loving relationship with a husband be part of "what is woman"?

The second part of Genesis 3:16, "*And* he will rule over you" (italics added), brings a fuller picture of the impact of the curse. This text in both Greek and Hebrew allows for either *and* or *but;* the context determines which one is to be chosen.[3] Assuming that both the "desire" *and* the "he will rule" are judgments of the curse, *and* would be the connecting word. However, if the woman's *desire* for her husband is a God-given *longing and attraction,* but as a result of sin, the fulfillment of this *desire* will be impeded, then the connecting conjunction would clearly be *but.* Our Scripture would read, "Your desire will be for your husband, *but* he will rule over you" (v. 16, italics added).

Down deep, a woman's heart longs for a beautifully romantic, warm, intimate relationship with a husband. This is not just a Cinderella syndrome (although it can become that); it is part of God's initial design for men and women to become "one flesh." But the impact of the Fall will now make that reality much more difficult. Men will rule over women. Sin will impede the most basic of societal relationships. Men will have difficulty being "considerate as

[they] live with [their] wives" and will fail to "treat them with respect as the weaker partners and heirs with [them] of the gracious gift of life" (1 Peter 3:7). Women will have difficulty responding in purity and reverence (v. 2).

Experience tells me this spills over into many male-female relationships. Men have difficulty understanding women, and women misunderstand men. Husbands, fathers, grandfathers, uncles, brothers, friends, neighbors, and coworkers impacted by sin *will rule over* women—and not with respect or understanding. Women, also impacted by sin, will not follow Peter's injunction to live in such a way that "if any do not believe the word, they may be won over without words by the behavior of their wives, when they see the purity and reverence of [their] lives" (vv. 1–2).

Part of the curse on the serpent, "I will put enmity between you and the woman, and between your offspring and hers" (Genesis 3:15), has been realized in every culture to some degree throughout history. Women are most often treated without respect as image bearers. Women have been degraded, marginalized, abused, and terrorized. When an evil tyrannical leader comes into power, often mistreatment of women is the first evidence. Why have we not been able to change this tide worldwide? Could it be a direct impact of this curse?

Another aspect of the mistreatment of women is a misunderstanding of the biblical expression "weaker partner" that we find in Peter. Through the years, many have described women as weaker emotionally, spiritually, physically, or mentally. However, in life and in Scripture, there are examples showing women's strength in each of these areas. Who can deny the strengths of judge-prophetess-leader Deborah or Mary mother of Jesus? Or modern-day Mother Teresa or Corrie ten Boom? Time and space prohibit a full list!

May I submit that the true meaning of "weaker partner" stems from the key definition of women as *life-bearer.* A woman's physiological makeup impacts her from puberty to postmenopause, and beyond. The monthly cycle a woman experiences most of her life brings a hormonal "weakness." Each month her body prepares to give life. Whether that preparation is rewarded with life or discarded, the impact can be felt emotionally, physically, and mentally, which may also affect her spiritually.

Whether a woman is married or single, her physiological make-up is the same. She is a life-bearer. This presents a vulnerability that elicits Peter's injunction for women to be treated with consideration, understanding, and respect. Incidentally, God, through Peter, would not have given this instruction were it not possible. It is possible to live with a woman in an understanding way. Doing so begins with understanding her high value in being a life-bearer and companion.

WOMaN IS DeSIÇNeD foR Life-ÇIVINÇ ReLatIONSHIPS

What is the essential nature of woman? She is at the core a life-bearer and a nurturer. She is a companion, one who comes alongside to enhance another. She was designed for life-giving relationships.

From conception to birth, from infancy to toddlerhood, from school age to adolescence, from college to career, in marriage and family or in single communities, women from the beginning were endowed with relational strengths. When sin entered the world through the Fall, those life-giving relationships became strained and difficult. Women receive injury and experience pain. Although the desires in the recesses of her heart remain the same, their fulfillment seems remote or elusive. She resorts to romance novels, movies, chat room relationships, and even affairs of her own making to fulfill her desire for love.

The good news is that even though God's ideal plan was clouded by the results of the Fall, God had a redemptive plan. That redemptive plan endears us to Him and to each other on a deep level. We begin to see a level of unconditional love that once we could only dream of experiencing. At times we still have difficulty believing it and embracing it fully, because we have not known such love on the human level. Yet we know it is truly how our heavenly Father feels about us. The high price of His Son's life given for us is evidence enough. Who else has loved us that much, to give up the very life-blood of His only Son, Jesus Christ!

Perhaps this sheds light on one of the most difficult texts for women in the Bible, 1 Timothy 2:15. Yes, the woman acknowledges she was deceived by the serpent (Genesis 3:13) while the man knowingly took the fruit. Our Timothy text tells us that the woman then became a sinner. "But," it says, "women will be saved through childbearing—if they continue in faith, love and holiness with propriety." Childbearing is painful. Child rearing is challenging at best. But women were de-signed to accept this challenge. Women have a nurturing interest, desire—even passion in some cases—to carry out these tasks. This may be played out in love for animals, gardening, or humans. This is God-designed. Although past abuse or pain may damage or diminish this ability to nurture, it is part of woman's original gender-design.

In the same way that we see Eve acknowledge her need for God as she becomes "the mother of all the living" for the first time, women who acknowledge their need for God in their life-giving role will "be saved." They will be fruitful in their life-giving relationships. God's desire for woman is that she develop godly character, and through that character generate and nurture life-giving relationships.

Three important aspects of godly character are named in 1 Tim-othy 2:15: "faith, love and holiness with propriety." It is amazing, the parallel of this with other key Scriptures for women. As we unpack these three elements of godliness, let's look at them in terms of women as life-givers: mothers, wives, and single women.

Let's begin with what many believe to be the core biblical in-struction for women.

the essential character of woman

Titus lived in a decadent society, Crete. Paul's description of the people who lived in this society will sound familiar to us.

For there are many rebellious people, mere talkers and deceivers. . . . They must be silenced, because they are ruining whole households by teaching things they ought not to teach—and that for the sake of dishonest gain. Even one of their own prophets has said, "Cretans are always liars, evil brutes, lazy gluttons." This testimony is true. . . . They claim to know God but by their actions they deny him. They are detestable, disobedient and unfit for doing anything good. (Titus 1:10–13, 16)

What did Paul ask Titus to do for greatest impact in the Cretan culture? First, he asked Titus to "appoint elders in every town" (1:5). Second, he asked Titus to teach that which reflects sound doctrine (2:1). Then in Titus 2:2–10 Paul asked Titus to teach four specific people-groups: (1) older men, (2) older women, (3) younger men, and (4) slaves. But one people group is missing from his list of people Titus himself should teach.

That people group is *younger women.* They are not included as recipients of Titus' teaching. Why not? Are they left out entirely? Will their impact in a decadent society not be felt? On the contrary! Two verses in this passage focus on training younger women (vv. 4–5). If the length of the passage is an indicator of their importance, then younger women are at the top of the list! All other people groups are given instructions in one verse only! Perhaps the old saying, "The hand that rocks the cradle rules the world," is actually biblical! The stories of Moses and Samuel certainly reflect the powerful impact of a mother's early influence on a child's life.

Then who is to train the younger women? *The older women!* But not just *any* woman who is older. The training should be done by women who are "reverent in the way they live, not to be slanderers or addicted to much wine, but to teach what is good. Then they can train the younger women" (Titus 2:3–4).

Let's look at these characteristics more closely. Are they any different from the requirements for the older men who are to teach? Look at the list of the four characteristics of the older men referred to in this passage and the parallel list for the older women (Figure 3.1).

Older men	Older women
1. Worthy of respect	1. Reverent in the way they live
2. Temperate	2. Not addicted
3. Self-controlled	3. Not slanderers
4. Sound in faith, love & endurance	4. Able to teach what is good

Figure 3.1

So many similarities! The list for older women begins with "likewise." This draws us back to the previous verse, which was the list for older men. The characteristics of the older men and the older women in this list are indeed alike! But when we see the characteristics of the older woman fleshed out in the life of a younger woman, we get a clearer picture of what those characteristics look like "with skin on." A godly older woman can best "translate" the teachings of godliness into the life of a younger woman. And certainly being pure, kind, self-controlled, and loving would not only impact the most intimate of relationships but *all* associations.

Do you wonder how this compares with the godly characteristics desired in the younger women? Let's add another column to the chart (Figure 3.2).

Older men	Older women	Younger women
1. Worthy of respect	1. Reverent in the way they live	1. Pure, kind
2. Temperate	2. Not addicted	2. Self-controlled
3. Self-controlled	3. Not slanderers	3. Self-controlled
4. Sound in faith, love & endurance	4. Able to teach what is good	4. Love their husbands and children; busy at home

Figure 3.2

What does this look like in the life of a young wife or mother? It will look like loving her husband and children so much that her primary focus in life will be those relationships. This is not saying that she will not have other interests or jobs in life. But it does say that God intentionally made her with the abilities she needs in these life-giving relationships. The teaching of the older women will enhance those abilities.

Compare this to the list given in 1 Timothy 3:11, describing deaconesses: "Women worthy of respect, not malicious talkers but temperate and trustworthy in everything." Does that list look familiar? It is essentially the same list! I love the summary characteristic: *trustworthy in everything.*

When you are looking for a friend, a mentor, or an older woman to help you, isn't this the ribbon that wraps up the entire package? Don't you want someone who is "trustworthy in everything"? A godly woman defined by the lists in Titus 2 and 1 Timothy 3 will be trustworthy in everything! An older woman who is able to teach what is good will teach by her life and words soundness in faith, love, and endurance. A younger woman who is taught by an older godly woman as described by Titus will become trustworthy.

What about single women? These same characteristics can flourish in a single woman. They can be "women worthy of respect, not malicious talkers but temperate and trustworthy in everything . . . reverent in the way they live" and teaching "what is good . . . self-controlled and pure . . . kind" (1 Timothy 3:11; Titus 2:3, 5). Godly single woman can have strategic impact on their culture. Their voices are needed, indeed, are paramount to impacting a decadent society for good.

The relationships of the older woman in our text are not identified. Although we imagine she was married and had children at some point in her life, the text does not say this. Many single women make important contributions to married women and moms. Many single women have a more expansive view of life and have the ability to stretch beyond familiar territory. Nurture and companionship enhance most relationships. The influence of single women in biblical times, such as Miriam, Mary Magdelene, Mary of Bethany, and Martha, is still being felt today.

THE IMPACT OF GODLY WOMEN
ON A DECADENT SOCIETY
Titus 1:10–16 and Titus 2:3–5
"We too were . . ." (Titus 3:3)

Now, let's contrast the characteristics of the decadent Cretan society with the godly characteristics Paul instructed Titus to encourage in women (Figure 3.3).

Cretans (Titus 1:10–16)	Before Christ	Godly women (Titus 2:3–5)
Rebellious people	Disobedient	Reverent living, kind (vv. 2, 5)
Mere talkers		Not to be slanderers (v. 3)
Deceivers	Deceived	Pure (v. 5)
Teaching what they should not for dishonest gain	Envy	Teach what is good (v. 3) Train the young women Word of God not maligned (v. 5)
Liars		Not to be slanderers (v. 3)
Evil brutes	Lived in malice (evil)	Pure, love husband, love child
Lazy gluttons	Enslaved by all kinds of passions and pleasures	Workers at home Reverent, pure
Minds and consciences corrupted		
Behavior ungodly	Foolish	Kind, temperate
Detestable	Hating and being hated	Kind, love husband, love child
Disobedient	Disobedient	Subject to husband
Unfit for doing anything good	Foolish	Sound in faith, love, and endurance!

Figure 3.3. Beverly Hislop

Do you see the import of this? The implications of Paul's instructions to Titus are powerful, and the impact of shepherding women in a decadent culture is profound! Older women are to teach younger women. Women, don't minimize your influence within your culture by ignoring this principle.

Now back to 1 Timothy 2:15. "But women will be saved through childbearing—if they continue in faith, love and holiness with propriety." Don't miss the similarity of these godly descriptions with our Titus 2 text: "Sound in faith, love and endurance . . . able to teach what is good. . . . Pure . . . kind . . . self-controlled."

To complete our list we must include 1 Peter 3. What insights does Peter give us regarding the essential character of a woman? Peter encourages women to influence others (specifically husbands) with their pure and reverent lives. Relationship is again the key. A woman should not rely on her outward beauty alone to send the message. Rather her greatest influence will be her inner self, "the unfading beauty of a gentle and quiet spirit, which is of great worth in God's sight" (v. 4). Further study of the words *gentle* and *quiet spirit* reveals an attitude that is available to women of all personalities and ages, single or married. It is an attitude that intentionally hears and obeys God.

A prize-winning horse chooses to bring itself under the direction of the jockey. The horse has incredible power and ability but chooses to submit those to its rider in order to win the race. Likewise, a woman chooses, with an accepting and gentle spirit, to bring herself under the direction of the Lord. This is highly valued by God! And good news, women: It does not fade with age! Needless to say, this inner beauty will be reflected in a woman's outward appearance. Peter assures us that women in the biblical past made themselves beautiful by the reflection of the "inner self," living a pure and reverent lifestyle in relationship.

summaRy

Being a godly woman is not easy but it *is* simple. As you compare the Scriptures addressing women, you will discover that the characteristics are relatively the same.

- The book of Titus declares that "women shepherding women" plays a key role in profoundly impacting a decadent culture for God.
- Paul names the life-giving aspect of womanhood as key to a woman's fulfillment (1 Timothy 2:15).
- First Peter 3 shows the value of a woman's living a pure and reverent life in relationship. Peter declares that living such a life is true, of lasting beauty, and of great worth in God's sight.

Two additional texts you may want to explore further clearly reflect the Scriptures we have already covered.

- The guidelines for church-supported widows include Titus 2 characteristics visible in a widow's family and community relationships (1 Timothy 5:9, 14).
- Proverbs 31, man's dream sheet for a godly wife (given by a mother-in-law-to-be!), reflects godly character as the essential ingredient that impacts family and community relationships. This proverb opens the door wider for a woman to move beyond her own household. But don't miss the key to her community success. It is an overflow of a strong, healthy, life-giving relationship with God and family, openly affirmed by her children and husband (v. 28).

How does this impact those who shepherd women? Both the Old and New Testaments reveal that from the beginning of time women were made to be nurturers. This necessitates relationship. Women naturally desire relationships. Women flourish best in relationships. This may be why it is so painful for a woman to experience conflict in relationship.

It is difficult for most women to focus on completing tasks with no thought of the people who are part of the process. Often a woman will *first* establish rapport with the people with whom she will work *before* she fully embraces the task. The relationship between the play-ers on a woman's baseball team is generally developed *before* the game. Men, on the other hand, consider a relationship between play-ers something that is established *while* or *because* they are playing the game—focusing on the same task together.

When a woman is in pain and in need of a shepherd, she re-sponds best to someone who extends care in a nurturing, relational manner. This shepherd is "speaking her language." Establishing some sort of relationship is critical to effective ongoing shepherding. This may be why women who so often speak of a spiritual leader who told them to "go home, read the Bible, and pray more," or "go home and love him more" were left further devastated in their pain. The focus in these statements is primarily *task* when what the woman needs is *a relational approach.*

Yes, Katrina, the Bible does reveal a difference in male and fe-male. It is the design of the Creator that women be life-bearers. As nurturers, women are endowed with special capacities to care for others. Women naturally want companionship. Women want to give and receive the benefits of intimacy with other human beings. And they do this best as they develop godly character.

Scripture clearly reflects that the original design of the Creator called for intentional male and female differences. The next chap-ter summarizes findings from the scientific community that mirror those differences.

4

INTERNAL UNDERSTANDING: ESSENCE OF WOMANHOOD

KELLIE WAS DISTRAUGHT. She was angry with Bill, only this time she was ready to walk out on him and the children. Life seemed broken with no hope of repair.

Stephanie had seen Kellie frustrated and confused before, but this was different. Kellie seemed to be making irrational judgments that had life-altering consequences. Stephanie tried to calm Kellie by sitting her down, getting her a cup of tea, and then listening. The more Kellie spoke, the more Stephanie wondered about the changes she was seeing in a longtime friend. Eventually Stephanie asked about Kellie's last medical checkup, strongly suggesting that Kellie make a new appointment.

Soon Kellie found that major hormonal changes were occurring in her body and were impacting her emotional responses. Once those changes were evaluated and addressed, Kellie was able to get a clearer perspective. With this new perspective, she was able to work toward restoring fragmented family relationships. Kellie's physiological condition was clearly impacting her psychological responses. Stephanie's understanding of those aspects of a woman's life enabled her to shepherd Kellie effectively.

To be effective in shepherding women we must be responsive to a woman's gender-specific characteristics, behaviors, and needs. To do that, we must understand what those characteristics are and how they are unique to women. First, this will involve looking at the physiological and psychological aspects of a woman's life. Second, this will involve identifying the characteristics of a woman's cognition and communication.

physiological aspects

Some ten years ago geneticist Anne Moir and journalist David Jessel set out—as many before them—to answer the question "Is there a real difference between men and women?" Moir, who had a Ph.D. in genetics, was to research the available data, while Jessel was to focus on writing up their findings in nonscientific language. Those conclusions, though not popular at the time, have been confirmed and expanded in myriad publications. Although this information is not new, it is important support for the premise of this book. It also echoes the biblical truth we have already explored: *Men and women are intentionally designed by their Creator to be different from one another from conception.*

Six to seven weeks after conception the brain begins to take on a male or female pattern. At this critical stage, the determined brain structure and organization will decide the very nature of the mind. The mother and the father each contribute half of the forty-six chromosomes to make up the genetic code of the child. In addition to the X or Y chromosomes, hormones are critical in sex determination. No matter the genetic makeup of the embryo, the fetus will only develop as a male if male hormones are present and female if female hormones are present. As early as six weeks, the male fetus develops the special cells that produce a colossal dose of male hormones, or androgens, mainly testosterone. These stimulate embryonic male genitalia. At puberty the male will receive a second such surge of male hormone.

At the same time, if the genetic code is XX, the fetus will continue on its path of developing female embryonic genitalia. "What matters is the degree to which our embryonic brains are exposed to male hormone. The less they get, the more the natural feminine mind-set will survive. . . . The die is cast in utero; that's when the mind is made up and the luggage of our bodies and of society's expectations of us merely supplement this basic biological fact of life."[1] Male hormone alters the way the brain network is laid. When it is present, the pattern is male. When it is absent, the pattern is female.

A woman's brain is structured differently from a man's. The two sides of her brain (corpus callosum) have a larger number of connections, which allows for more information to be exchanged. This allows a woman to better recognize the emotional nuances in voice, gesture, and facial expression. She can deduce more from such information than a man can because she has a greater capacity to integrate verbal and visual information. A woman is less able to separate emotion from reason because the emotional side of her brain is more integrated with the verbal side.[2] A woman integrates all the issues in problem solving. To disconnect them seems like denial. This is why a woman is typically better at multitasking.[3]

A woman is more alert to touch, smell, and sound. She is better at imparting and receiving the social cues of body languages. She sees more. A woman literally uses greater eye contact and faces another woman more directly when talking. Women see, hear, and feel more, and what they receive means more to them. "She understands better than a man, what a man or woman means even when he or she is apparently saying nothing. . . . The intuitive, if you like, is more in touch with the communicative skills."[4] A woman may cry more often because she receives more emotional input, reacts more strongly to it, and expresses it with greater force.

A man finds it more difficult to express his emotions because the information he is receiving flows less easily to the verbal side of his brain.[5] The man is more single-minded because his brain is more compartmentalized. He does not notice distractions. "His, since birth, has been the world of things. . . . This leads him to tackle problems in a practical, overall, inherently self-interested manner. . . . Men, with their 'doing' brains, will respond to another's distress by searching for a practical solution to it. . . . The circuit board of the male brain is programmed for action rather than people. It ignores megabytes of personal information, such as the delicate visual cues to which women respond so much more readily in conversation."[6]

While the sex of the brain is determined at the time of neural organization in the womb, the difference of brain sex fully shows with the onset of the hormones in puberty. A woman receives a high level of "oxytocin, a hormone that supports not only lactation but, apparently, bonding and nurturing behaviors."[7] This will stimulate the need and desire to form and maintain close relationships with the people around her.

Certainly there will be characteristic variations from woman to woman and man to man. Personality differences, experiences, education, and talents will play into male and female peculiarities. Exceptions to these patterns will be obvious. Variations in hormonal levels at six weeks from conception, at puberty, and at menopause will contribute greatly to these apparent exceptions. Some of these issues are controversial. Yet there are observable generalities directly attributed to gender.

Little controversy centers on the fact that a woman's biological structures are uniquely female, not shared in the male experience. "We are different anatomically, hormonally, socially, sexually, psychologically and emotionally. God created men and women as two distinct pieces of a puzzle."[8] The rhythms of menstruation, breast development, pregnancy, giving birth, lactation, and menopause certainly impact a woman's life. "There are times when being a woman just plain hurts. At any age from puberty to menopause, menses can be the source of extreme discomfort. . . . 3.5 million have symptoms so severe that they are unable to function for one to two days each month."[9]

Estrogen has a critical impact on the activity of the human brain in both men and women through all the life cycles. Dr. Barbara Sherwin, professor of psychology and obstetrics-gynecology at McGill University in Montreal, has been doing studies over a period of nearly ten years on women in all stages of life. The results are clear, says Sherwin. "Estrogen helps maintain verbal memory and it enhances a woman's capacity for new learning."[10] "The general midlife decrease of estrogen increases memory challenges in women. This can be frustrating to a woman who has learned to count on her mental acuities in younger years. Although hormone replacement therapy (HRT) may augment this loss, it creates new physical risks."[11]

Although the physical aspects of these experiences can be painful, the emotional implications may bring greater concern. The change in estrogen and progesterone levels can impact every aspect of a woman's life. The emotional uncertainties impact relationships and are an ongoing concern for women. Monthly hormone changes are a regular consideration in understanding women. It may be difficult to document the enormous impact of these physiological distinctives in a woman's life. Fortunately for Kellie, Stephanie understood these irregularities and urged Kellie to get the assessment she needed.

Women certainly bring deeper understanding to women with the physiological issues that define womanhood. Who can understand the pain of childbirth but someone who has also pushed, cried, screamed, and rejoiced? Who can enter into the monthly blues or serious PMS depression better than one who has also clawed the couch or let out a scream or two? Who could relate to the horror of falling from the pinnacle of joy at the birth of a new baby into the hole of depression and thoughts of murder or suicide? Menopause symptoms do not sound reasonable to someone who has not repeatedly wakened in the middle of the night soaked—and startled— resulting in serious sleep deprivation. The risks of taking hormonal replacements may appear to be a senseless game of roulette, unless the intensity of wakeful nights, hot flashes, vaginal dryness, and erratic menstrual cycles are a known experience.

SEASONS of LIFE

Hormonal changes often create asymmetry in a given season of life. It seems that just as biology triggers new confusing feelings, relational and environmental factors transition also. Often there are multiple influences, simultaneous changes in a woman's life that cause stress and pain. Identifying a woman's stage of life is important to understanding the whole picture.

The focus of this book does not allow for detailed descriptions of each season of a woman's life. However, overall exposure to the seasons of a woman's life is helpful in offering good pastoral care. The point to be made is that shepherds should understand that "the model of male adult development should not be univocally applied to women and that relationship and autonomy can be integrated within adults but differently for men and women."[12]

Carl Jung (1875–1961) was one of the earliest writers on lifelong psychological development. Jung's essay "The Stages of Life" (1933) planted seeds of much of the understanding of midlife today. His central theme was that the qualities or interests in the first half of life would be changed into the opposite qualities in midlife.[13]

Building on Jung's study, Daniel Levinson followed his text on men with adaptations for women. Daniel Levinson simply defined *adolescing* as "growing up," a positive growth toward optimum potential moving toward adulthood. *Senescing* is "growing down," a negative growth and dissolution, moving toward old age. Midlife is the hill between the two.[14] While Levinson identifies five stages of development in adult life, Charles Sell and Gail Sheehy narrow it to three: Young (provisional) adulthood (18–30), Middle (first) Adulthood (30–45), and Older (second) Adulthood (45–85, or until death).[15] Although developmental studies on youth have long been in place, only recently has expanded study on adulthood taken place. As life expectancy figures rise, more research is warranted on the upper end of adulthood.

Another model of "family life cycles" defines seven stages determined by offspring: (1) Young couples without children; (2) child-bearing families and families with children in the preschool years; (3) families with school-age children; (4) families with adolescents in the home; 5) launching families; (6) empty nest families; (7) families in retirement. The stage of the oldest child determines the family life cycle.[16] This model can be helpful in understanding the source and level of stress for the family of each stage. For example, the School-Aged stage shows the highest level of stress for the family centered on the increased number of "outside activities." The greatest family financial strain peaks out in the Adolescent Stage. The highest level of stress due to transitions falls in the Launching Stage. The strains of each stage greatly impact a woman.

Olson documents the emotional responses of women and men through development stages. The greatest distance between husband and wife across all seven stages is in acquiring social support (outside the family). In every stage wives initiated and received significantly more social support than the husbands.[17] The assumption can be drawn that in all seasons of life women feel a greater need for relational connection and support.

Often a woman going through the emotional ups and downs of menopause will typically be in the launching or empty nest stage. With a ten-year shift in life stages from the 1950s to 1990s, adolescence is often extended into the late twenties.[18] Often the turbulence of these years for a woman coincides with premenopause or menopause and caring for aging parents.

Gail Sheehy's work provides a more comprehensive model of understanding of life cycles for men and women individually.[19] Throughout each decade of life, women "process" differently than men, although that difference will vary across the life map.

For the first ten years of life, males and females share many similarities. At puberty the genders diverge dramatically. The greatest distinction between the sexes occurs in the late thirties. In the mid-fifties male and female similarities again converge, with males taking on more female attributes and females taking on male attributes.[20] Men often become more expressive and emotionally responsive.

Women may become more independent and assertive. "What is now known biochemically is that the ratio of 'female' sex hormone (estrogen) to 'male' sex hormone (testosterone) decreases markedly as women reach middle life."[21] Women continue producing testosterone even after their ovaries have stopped making estrogen. The ratio of testosterone to estrogen in a postmenopausal woman may be up to twenty times higher than in a woman who is still ovulating. In a man the levels shift in the opposite direction, although "males will always have at least ten times as much testosterone as females."[22]

During these transitional times, puberty and menopause, most women have the greatest difficulty embracing the hormonal changes. Although the age-old question of nature or nurture is still debated, many environmental issues combine with genetic patterns to impact these critical stages of life.[23] Each cycle brings a file of challenges. Identifying a woman's physiological season (noting hormonal activity) and family life cycle (demands of children, husband, and extended family) will lend more insight and understanding to her needs. Certainly all of these models bring elements of understanding that enhance our ability to shepherd women.

PSYCHOLOGICAL aspects

A second area of understanding is the psychological aspect of a woman's life. The study of psychology of women within the science of psychology is a relatively young field of study, although much has been contributed in the last thirty years. For many years the healthy adult model was defined by the characteristics of a healthy adult male.[24]

The writings of Sigmund Freud powerfully impacted psychotherapy for women. The Freudian theory of penis envy, identifying a woman's basic problem as shame and envy due to a lack of a penis, clearly reflects a male perspective. In Freud's studies the mentally healthy woman appeared as passive, dependent, childlike, and resigned to her biologically inferior status. Freud further concluded that because women never fully resolved the Oedipus complex, their final level of moral development was not as advanced as a man's. Women were clearly inferior to men.[25]

Later psychological development was built on the foundation Freud laid. For example, Lawrence Kohlberg's initial study on the stages of moral development[26] was based on the responses of eighty-four boys whose development was followed over a period of twenty years. These findings were presented as universal human responses. Women measured on this scale were judged deficient in moral maturity because they responded at lower levels than the males.[27] These reinforced cultural stereotypes have shaped the thinking of professionals (largely, though not exclusively, male) for decades. Gender differences were relegated to misunderstandings of the psychological characteristics of women. Therapy models were male models. These assumptions continued to be reinforced in society, filtering into the Christian community.

As the study of the psychology of women grew, the debate over gender differences versus similarities continued. Therapists argued men and women were so different that women are the "absolute other." Women should live by different rules and function differently in relationship. Later debate insisted men and women were the same and should abide by the same rules, roles, and functions in relationship. Of course neither brings a totally accurate conclusion. In some ways women and men are more alike than different; in other ways they are more different than alike.[28]

Feminist history reflects this debate. In the first wave (1848–1920), feminists simply wanted equal access to the rights to vote, own property, and have educational opportunities. Women admittedly were seen as different than men. Their primary focus was to gain a social voice to directly impact areas of concern to women. Women identified specific areas (social, political, economical) in which they campaigned for equal access. The second wave in the 1960s declared that the accepted differences of women and men were actually viewed as weaknesses. So the agenda was to become just like men. Feminists insisted that women were as capable as men to make sound decisions, to earn advanced degrees, and to work in professions previously held by men. Women worked to overcome sex distinctions. Feminist women began to dress, act, and work like men. The third wave in the 1970s saw the agenda intensify as feminists began to see women's differences as a source of pride, leading to an agenda of female superiority. Feminists soon moved to a place of "re-imaging," redefining themselves, and intentionally eradicating any need for male presence.[29]

What are the solid conclusions about gender specific characteristics given the plethora of contradictory messages?

The dictionary defines psychology as the "science of human and animal behavior."[30] As psychologists continue to research and draw conclusions about patterns of human behavior, their findings will reflect elements of truth. We can gain from these findings patterns that assist us in understanding how humans respond to myriad stimuli. We are able to chart predictable responses, overt actions of both males and females. Helpful insights can be gained from careful analysis of the elements women experience that bring them to a place of emotional healing from trauma. A wise steward of truth assimilates findings from many disciplines into a biblically sound conclusion.

The biblical truth of God's purpose in creating male and female to fully reflect His image will prevail. God intentionally created two different genders, with unique purpose for each. There are similarities and differences in both purpose and design.

Our purpose in this book is to draw findings from many of the arenas that impact a woman's life, to intentionally identify the unique characteristics, behaviors, and needs of a woman, for the greater purpose of providing truly effective pastoral care. Often the prevalent opinion in a culture permeates the church, consciously or subconsciously. The church reflects the controversy felt in both psychology (the study of human behavior) and sociology (the study of human society) because the people in the church are part of that cultural composition.

It is clear that women were created as different from men. Women are life-bearers, nurturers. Relationship is a primary concern for women. These differences have been observed in the pastoral counseling setting by Jim Smith, who observes that "the depth of differences between men and women is profound."[31] Here is a listing of some of those differences:

1. **Women, single and married, struggle more with relational issues than men.**

For that reason women seek marital counseling much more often than men. "Men tend to wrestle more with problems in their career and less with problems at home. In fact a man can tolerate a fairly low degree of marital happiness if his career is moving forward. Women cannot."[32]

This reflects the focus of the Genesis 3 curse. Men feel the impact specifically in the daily tasks of their work. The focus for women is on relationships. Women appear to establish basic identity through relationships of intimacy and nurture that are different from those of men.[33] Studies of developmental processes conclude that masculinity is primarily defined through processes of separation, while femininity is defined through attachment.[34] Women appear to differ from males in their continuing adult need for affiliation and intimacy.[35]

This may have greater implications than noted at first glance. A woman's sense of self, of who she is, is organized around being able to make and maintain relationships. Developing relationships will be valued as highly as or higher than self-improvement or power. The impact of this threat of disrupting connection is perceived not as just a loss of relationships but as something closer to a total loss of self.[36] Maintaining connections with others can be life giving to women, while loss can be life threatening. In patterns of male development, separation and power are most important. Men certainly desire relationships but are primarily drawn to establish separation and power. These are more often encountered in career and are of high priority to men.

A first priority for women in the marketplace is to establish relational alliances.

Empathy, mutuality, and self-boundaries have special significance to women. Women want to define the relationship with people around them; women need to know how they stand in relationship to coworkers before they move forward in corporate strategies.

There is a greater recognition of the need for more people-oriented skills in management. These are skills women have been taught to cultivate since they were little girls. Marilyn Loden asserts that the key interpersonal skills called for in marketplace leadership are those "frequently identified as more finely developed in feminine leaders":

1) *Sensing skills*—The ability to pick up on non-verbal cues, to understand the feelings and reactions of others.

2) *Listening skills*—Paying close attention to what is being said and how it is being stated. Letting people finish their thoughts without interrupting.

3) *Management of feelings*—Being attuned to one's feelings and to environmental conditions that trigger various feelings. Using one's own feeling reactions as an emotional barometer within group settings.

4) *Intimacy/authenticity*—Developing personal rapport with others. Sharing personal data about oneself and encouraging others to do this. Focusing on the whole individual, not just the employee.

5) *Soliciting feedback*—Soliciting feedback from colleagues and employees. Using feedback to modify one's behavior.

6) *Assessing personal impact*—Recognizing how one is being perceived and the consequences of one's actions on relationship building.[37]

The female temperament "lends itself to nurturance, caring, sensitivity, tenderness and compassion. . . . She is especially good at reading the character of people."[38] Certainly the marketplace recognizes the interpersonal effectiveness of implementing these skills. The distinction between marketplace personnel and church personnel is narrowing. The majority of the women in our churches spend their waking hours in that marketplace, either full-time or part-time.[39] Women attending our churches are using these skills in arenas outside the church. Would it not make sense that the body of Christ should also benefit from these God-given abilities?

The majority of women responding to a denominational sample questionnaire did perceive gender to be in some way an influencing factor in their shepherding experiences. "The positive factors were that women are better listeners, are more empathic, more approachable, more nurturing, more relational, more comfortable with the expression of feelings and are interested in women's growth and empowerment."[40]

The implications are powerful in shepherding women. Since relationship is a defining entity, generally more important than power or independence in a woman's life, she needs input from someone who understands or shares this perspective. This woman wants above all to develop a healthy interdependence and a stronger connection. A healthy shepherd will employ strong listening, sensing, feedback, and assessing skills, while using emotional barometers and personal rapport.

2. Women usually want support and understanding.

So the ministry of presence is a *lot* more important to women than it is to men. When men come in, they expect a solution, a report.[41] Women tend to come for counseling earlier in their problem.

Women work out their moral dilemmas in terms of relational issues in a way different from the abstract principles utilized by men.[42] Clearly there is a different expectation and predicable delivery. Women want to talk, and they want to be listened to. Men, given a choice, may pick actions over words. They would rather do something than talk about it.[43] Perhaps this is the reason so many women feel marginalized by men in leadership. Fortunately this is not true of all men in leadership. Although leaders who do take this approach do so from a gender-induced response (rather than with an intentionally devaluing purpose), most women will feel devalued because their feelings have been discredited, discounted. Instead shepherds who intentionally provide emotional support and understanding open the door for further healing.

3. Women feel excessively responsible for others.

Men are self-absorbed, more insensitive to even their own needs. These are at the extreme ends of a mental health continuum.[44]

In Kohlberg's study of moral development, women appear to be stuck at stage three, making decisions on the basis of pleasing and helping others, rather than abstract rights and universal principles. As stated earlier, Kohlberg's scale was developed in a study using all male subjects. Carol Gilligan, a former student of Kohlberg, found that women reason differently than men about moral issues. The moral reasoning of women, according to Gilligan, centers on responsibility and conflicting human relationships. Women's sense of integrity becomes intertwined with an *ethic of care* and responsibility expressed over their life span. Women reflect their priority that no one should be hurt.[45]

The strength of a woman's healthy sense of care for others makes her an ideal candidate for shepherding others. Clearly Gilligan's study reflects the God-given ability to nurture. Women were created to give care, to sense relationship needs within and without the home.

Once again, women and men approach pain from opposite perspectives. Ideally, when both genders are operating from a place of health, this will bring balance. However, in the midst of emotional pain, this difference can inhibit pastoral care. While women are pressing for men to become more sensitive and responsible, men are insistent that women need to "let it go" or "forget it." A woman often feels devalued, discounted when she receives this response. She needs to hear a response that gives support and understanding to her concern, because the issue inevitably involves a relationship and thus is very important to her.

Understanding the life-giving or life-threatening nature of

relationships to women places a shepherd in place of maximum effectiveness. Women need to realize they are only responsible *for* themselves, although they may be responsible *to* others. The only person a woman has the power to change is herself. Woman's natural affinity toward connectedness may be one of God's reasons for declaring, "it is not good for man to be alone," if in fact man is inclined toward self-absorption. A woman who is psychologically healthy, who has decidedly taken responsibility for her own growth and maturity, is in the best position to influence even the self-absorbed toward a middle posture on the health continuum. After all, Eve's presence brought completion to a man whose Creator declared "not good" in his aloneness.

4. Women put feelings before thoughts.

Women cannot think about their options, about what they ought to do until they have first worked through their feelings. Women often cry but seldom apologize for it. On the other hand, men tend to put their feelings on hold until they have had a chance to get their thoughts on the table. They put thoughts before feelings. Men are afraid they will break down emotionally during counseling. When men do cry, they usually apologize.[46]

Women need the freedom to emotionally process their feelings —to cry. Many men are uncomfortable with tears and feel helpless in the presence of a woman crying. Men feel a need to stop the tears and enter into a productive discussion that will provide a clear solution to the problem. Certainly a woman needs someone to help her think through her options. A woman needs to make a well-thought-through decision regarding her next step to bring logical thought into this process. However, the *order* of this process is often ignored. A woman cannot easily think about the options until she has worked through her feelings.

5. Women manage stress with a relational response.

Women are more likely to manage their stress with what Pennsylvania State professor Dr. Laura Cousino Klein describes as a "tend-and-befriend" response by nurturing their children or seek-ing social contact, especially with other women.[47] This is a sharp contrast to the fight-or-flight behavior of men. The hormone oxy-tocin is thought to be the key. Studies show "that oxytocin decreases anxiety and depression, and promotes an affiliation or friend-seek-ing response in females," Klein reports. "After a hard day's work women are more likely to affiliate, while men may need time to de-compress. Both men and women produce oxytocin from the poste-rior pituitary gland, but women churn out more."[48]

In summary, women clearly focus on relational issues more than men. Women are particularly good at reading the character of peo-ple, of leading relationally, and of functioning from an ethic of care.

WOMeN'S COGNItION

Another critical area of understanding is how women know and process knowledge. Often we can assume all women respond the same way to receiving information, finding truth, and making life changes. This is not the case. Mary Field Blenky, Blythe McVicker Clinchy, Nancy Rule Goldburger, and Jill Mattuck Tarule have iden-tified women's five ways of knowing.

1. *Silence*—These women do not have the ability to speak for themselves. They accept any external authority blindly. They are mindless and voiceless. These women submit to any voice of authority, even when that authority brings harm. There is no confidence in learning from words. Words are weapons and these women worry they will be punished for using words.

2. *Received knowledge*—These women cannot see themselves as coming up with knowledge on their own. They listen to the voice of others for self-knowledge. They believe what someone in a powerful position says about them. They see

everything as black or white, no gray. There is only one right answer. They tend to make literal interpretations. They collect facts, not opinions.

3. *Subjective knowledge*—These women reject outside authority. They *only* listen to inner voices. They become their own authority—which is dangerous. As children, their external authorities betrayed their trust, failed them. This led them to realize that they were capable of thinking on their own. They perceive firsthand experience as having the greatest value. They distrust logic and analysis.

4. *Procedural knowledge*—Women in this category invest in knowledge. They know truth must be ferreted out. They can either follow a pattern of separateness (impersonal) or connectedness (relational). Those who are separatists are suspicious of all truth. Everyone, including self, could be wrong. They set out to find the hole. On the other hand, connected women believe truth is found in relationship. They want to understand others and access their knowledge.

5. *Constructed knowledge*—These women are creators of knowledge. They are able to integrate emotion and mind. They allow the inner and outer world tapes to play simultaneously. This woman is a whole person. She has a passion for learning and is enticed by complexity. She is able to relate to others, to empathize, and is sensitive to the interior life of others.

Women have strong cognitive abilities. Certainly a list of women who exhibit strong cognitive skills in every discipline could be quickly compiled. The differences reflected in the above list are not in cognitive ability, rather in the developmental stage of ability. Many women stay in one category all their lives. Only with strong support and encouragement do women move from one category to another. Age is not a factor.[49]

Vicki wondered why Betty seemed to listen so intently, offering little response to questions. No matter how insistent Vicki was that Betty express her feelings, Betty declined. Rather, Betty clearly just wanted advice from Vicki. Once Vicki realized that Betty's way of knowing was silence, Vicki was able to explore the possibility of past and present abuse in Betty's life. Women like Betty have been raised to believe they should not speak or have an opinion of their own. Rather they submissively accepted the authoritarian words and abuse of their parents. While fully 75 percent of the silent and received knowers depicted one or both of their parents as alcoholic, only 2 percent of the reflective and constructive knowers combined gave a parent this label.[50]

On the other hand, Aida freely expressed her feelings and thoughts to Connie. Aida welcomed Connie's empathy and questions. Aida did not simply want advice. She wanted someone to "coach" her to discover workable solutions to the strained relationship with her brother. Aida realized that no one knew her brother and herself in quite the way she did. She needed to discover a solution that took into consideration the feelings of her family and her own desire to resolve this conflict. Aida had the ability to integrate feeling and cognition, to construct knowledge.

Once again we are reminded that although there are some true generalities about women, women do not all process life alike. Once these differences are identified, women can be more effectively shepherded according to their way of knowing.

COMMUNICATION

Women and men who live or work together have experienced the challenge of successfully communicating with each other. Deborah Tannen's research reveals clear differences in the communicative patterns and styles of women and men.[51] Understanding these differences will enhance pastoral care.

According to Tannen, for women language is primarily a way of establishing connections, interdependence, and negotiating relationship. Women want to establish closeness, sameness, and symmetry; to minimize differences and reach consensus. Men, on the other hand, see language primarily as a means to preserve independence and negotiate status. Men want to establish separateness, differences, and asymmetry.[52]

Tannen further notes that for women conflict is a real threat to connection and to be avoided at all costs. For men, conflict is the necessary means by which independence and status are negotiated, so it is accepted. As we have already noted, in problem solving women want understanding, feelings confirmed, and the sense of community strengthened. Men want to solve the problem; asymmetry frames the advice giver as more knowledgeable. Women do more "rapport-talking," private speaking, using personal examples when speaking. Men more often do "report-talking," public speaking, using knowledge, and skills.[53] Men will usually try to figure things out on their own, whereas women will readily ask for help. Women tend to personalize rejection more than men.[54]

In faculty meetings, Heather observes that men, after strongly disagreeing about the particular issue on the table, are able to shake hands and leave the room without questioning their established relationship with one another. Heather, on the other hand, feels a need to give and receive affirmation from her colleagues after a heated debate. What appears to be a "good discussion" to her male colleagues feels like tension-filled conflict to Heather, something she would rather avoid.

In summary, Tannen found that women use language to create community and men use language to manage contest.[55] Is it any wonder there is so much misunderstanding among women receiving pastoral care from male leaders? Can we see the beautiful intent of Creator God in making us different, while living with the tensions of those differences? There are clearly areas women are best equipped to minister to women, while men bring complementary aspects. The challenge is to identify these differences and give women the tools and permission needed to respond with confidence to the biblical injunctions for shepherding women! Hopefully some of the elements of this book will contribute to that process.

summary

A shepherd of women is the best candidate to provide primary pastoral care to another woman. Psychologically women understand women. Women are relationally focused and desirous of understanding and support. Emotional processing precedes decision making. Physiologically, only women experience the emotional and hormonal unpredictability of being a life-bearer. Women understand on a level that men cannot. These understandings come naturally to most women because the Creator made women as nurturers, life-bearers. Women's ways of knowing open the door for women to integrate the emotional and cognitive aspects of life-producing wholeness. In the absence of constructed knowledge women are at risk without voice, opinion, and truth. This vulnerability may be minimized as other women come alongside, leading the way in community, rather than contest. Women certainly are better able to communicate with women in similar venues, enhancing the connection that is so essential for women.

Effective pastoral care to women incorporates the scriptural concepts that women and men are of equal value and women's femininity is equally vital and necessary (as is a man's masculinity) in the human task of imaging God; that women are equally capable and responsible to manage their lives in obedience to the will of God; that equal in value does not require sameness in characteristic behavior or need.

Healthy shepherding encourages a woman to value, even highlight her femininity, her uniqueness as a woman in God's family. It will enable a woman to integrate womanhood and personhood in a way that realizes God's best for her.

Cultural and historical backdrops directly impact that ability to highlight a woman's feminine nature. Understanding external changes in women's lives will further define strategic shepherding.

5

external understanding: backdrop of pastoral care to women

SOCIETAL AND HISTORICAL changes for women have certainly increased in the last century. As we look at the external backdrop of women in today's world, we can see the increase in emotional pain worldwide. Surely this condition highlights the urgency for women to shepherd women.

TRENDS FOR WOMEN IN THE UNITED STATES

The early years of colonization in America took incredible fortitude. Women and men left everything to come to this continent and to trek across the wide expanse of the New World. Men and women worked together to provide everything for daily living, overcoming incredible odds. Death was common. The task of living was too large for a single parent, and so marriages often took place for survival. A man and a woman brought skill and ability to the other that would mean staying alive in the cold of winter and heat of summer.

Agrarian Society

For much of human history men and women worked together, complementing each other's work. The farmer's wife was just as important as the farmer. Children would help parents where they could. Often neighbors or relatives came in to care for the children while Mom made candles and soap, spun the cloth, or processed fresh crops. Women helped each other with quilting, canning, and other large chores. They visited as they worked and offered each other encouragement and care. They brought comfort and practical help at births and deaths. There was a sense of community, of connection. Women instinctively shepherded each other.

Industrial Society

The industrial revolution brought great change to the American family. Men earned income in exchange for hours worked away from home. Poor women went into the factories or did domestic work. Work that brought a paycheck and social recognition suddenly was work done outside of the home. Although many women were drawn into the workforce during World War II, after the war there was an organized effort to remove women from the factories and machine shops so that soldiers returning to civilian life had job opportunities.

As recently as 1964 it was perfectly legal for employers to respond to a female job applicant with "We don't hire women to do that." Although it took a while for the impact to be felt, the 1964 Civil Rights Act changed the world for women and men. Women have always done what needed to be done with multitask ability. Now, at least theoretically, women had recognition and could not be denied opportunities in politics, medicine, law, the military, entrepreneurial business, and other traditionally male areas of employment.

After the Industrial Revolution what women did at home began to lose its value. Nurturing was no longer seen as worth a woman's time, and women looked down on those women who depended on their husbands for income. They questioned a woman's not using her education in a career outside the home. The message: To have worth, you must work like a man.

The stay-at-home-mom occupation was further diminished in the eyes of society at large. As more and more women entered the workforce, the full-time nurturers felt more and more isolated. Neighborhoods were empty during the day. Children had fewer children on their own street with whom to play. The women who stayed at home felt increasingly isolated and felt a chasm between themselves, friends, and neighbors who did not share their commitment to nurture the next generation as a full-time career. In defense of this important career, they identified their role as "work *inside* the home" as opposed to "work *outside* the home."

The isolation of working women also increased because of fewer discretionary hours. Women who were once friends felt the impact of this tension. Societal structures moved women from a place of interdependent collaboration and community to a place of isolation, of disconnectedness from one another.

Today women have to be intentional about finding ways to enter community, to connect with one another. The need for input, care, and shepherding from other women is heightened even further because these kinds of relationships are not readily available. They are not built into the everyday life of most women.

Information Society

Women have entered new arenas of mission and discovery and achieved great accomplishments, both nationally and internationally. The number of women employed outside the home continues to increase (as high as two-thirds of all U.S. adult women are employed, and three-fourths of all employed women are working full time). More than six in ten women in the U.S. workforce have children younger than three.[1]

The number of female-headed households continues to rise. The contemporary woman leads life without margins—there is no room for error or the unexpected. Although she is rich in opportunities,

she is poor in time resources. Baby boomers were the first generation to have lifelong careers outside the home.[2]

Researchers Liz Nickles and Laurie Ashcraft documented this
significant social shift in three surveys conducted in the 1970s,
1980s, and 1990s titled *Update: Women.* In the late 1970s only about
half of women ages 20–50 worked outside the home. In the late
1990s three-quarters of the women ages 20–50 worked. In the 1970s
women drew an attitudinal line in the sand, working woman vs.
homemaker. Both felt strongly about their position and didn't hesi-
tate to express their views in moral terms. Women in the 1980s were
trying to "do it all" and were expressing increased stress. This gave
rise to stress-relief industries, clubs, and groups. By the late 1990s
the attitudinal differences between working and nonworking women
subsided. As the new millennium dawned, women generally were
less career driven and more focused on home and the relationships
therein. Cottage industries, flextime, and job sharing increased. The
development of e-commerce and telecommunication opened the
door for women to spend fewer hours at the office, while providing income from home.[3]

However, this did not eliminate the stressful demands of employment. It merely brought it into the home. It may have saved
commute time, but it made it more difficult for women to separate
home and work. Instead of home being a haven from the hurried-
ness of life, it became Grand Central Station, complete with in-
stant communication and the demands of clients and supervisors
for a quick response.

Nearly every gain has a downside; everything is a trade-off. For
women, though the achievements and opportunities have increased,
so have the mental, emotional, and spiritual needs. Placed alongside
this are increased isolation and disconnection from other women.
Some women have tasted control in the workplace and liked the fla-
vor. Other women have scars from the battles fought to gain what
the law provided. Pioneers often felt like "loners" because of time
spent in new vistas without models or companions.

This tension increased the potential for emotional or physical abuse for children living in the home. Couple this with a spouse who contributed a second set of career demands in the home, or a mother who carried these tensions alone. Emotional and physical abuse toward children and women in the American family has increased. Stress is at an all-time high. The physical, emotional, mental, and spiritual needs of women may be greater than at any previous time in the history of the United States. There may have been more traumatic circumstances in the lives of American women, but there probably has not been a time when women have had fewer helpful connections and less effective shepherding.

global trends for women

Worldwide there is an increase in physical and sexual abuse affecting millions of girls and women, yet known to be seriously unreported. In national studies in eleven countries, the proportion of women who report having been abused by an intimate partner at some point in their lives ranges from 5 to 48 percent. Localized studies in Africa, Latin America, and Asia report higher rates of physical violence—up to 58 percent of women.[4] One study in Brazil found that 60 percent of women homicide victims were killed by an intimate partner.[5] A current or former partner commits 61–78 percent of female homicides in Ontario, Canada,[6] whereas the statistic is 30 percent in the United States.[7] There are no accurate statistics of "honor killings," male family members killing women or girls suspected of behavior regarded as shameful or dishonoring. These murders occur with no legal reprisal.[8]

In India there is blatant abuse of female babies and girls, who are distinctly less valued than males. "There are more passive forms of female neglect, sustained nutritional deprivation and delayed health care for female infants. . . .Today female infanticide has emerged in a new form—sex-selective abortions."[9]

In some African countries as high as 98 percent of the women have undergone female genital mutilation.[10] In Egypt, 100 percent of the women with no education and 91 percent of the women with a secondary education have undergone female genital mutilation—and "its prevalence is not declining."[11] "Women and girls comprise half of the world's refugees and, as refugees, are particularly vulnerable to sexual violence while in flight, in refugee camps, and/or during resettlement."[12]

Women account for 46 percent of the adults currently living with HIV/AIDS. Almost 70 percent of the global total of HIV-positive people live in sub-Saharan Africa, and 55 percent of those are women. In southern and southeastern Asia, 30 percent of adults with HIV/AIDS are women.[13] A woman's risk of becoming infected with HIV during unprotected sexual intercourse is two to four times higher than that of a man. Social and cultural factors increase women's vulnerability to HIV.[14] In some cultures, women must remain monogamous while it is accepted that husbands have many sexual partners. Wives feel powerless to monitor their own safe sex. Women carry the burden of ill health and having to earn income while raising fatherless children.

Globally, women's share of the labor force has increased almost everywhere. In South America and southern Asia 45 percent of the workforce are women. Women comprise 62 percent of the labor in sub-Saharan Africa and 55 percent in developed regions (Europe, Australia, Japan, New Zealand, Canada, Bermuda, and the United States). The lowest recorded rates are for women in Arab countries, where cultural and social factors tend to discourage women's work outside the home.[15]

Women's increased participation in the labor force is accredited to the result of more control over their fertility, changes in public attitudes, and in some places, policies that are more favorable toward women. Expansion of the service sector, which employs more women, is also a factor in many countries. More women in Europe and North America are remaining in the labor force throughout their childbearing years. The previous pattern was a withdrawal from the labor force during reproductive years. African and Asian women have always remained in the labor force while having children. Economic and health factors are great contributors to the need for these women to work.

While some women globally have more marketplace opportunity, most face extreme family and societal pressures and pain. Gender discrimination, HIV/AIDS virus, genital mutilation (which is seen at an increased rate in U.S. immigrants), refugee risks and poverty, and violent crimes against women are only a few of the issues women deal with every day. Forced prostitution, extreme poverty, illiteracy, death, atrocities within the home, forced abortions, and a lack of health facilities only lengthen the list of painful issues our sisters around the world must face. Fundamentalist Islamic extremists forbid women to do commercial work, even in their homes. They are secluded at home and are without educational or social opportunities.[16] Hindu women are valued in society only by their service to men and birthing sons. Muslim women in rich Arab countries may have Ph.D.'s and big stock portfolios yet not be allowed to drive cars or go out without a male companion or a veil. Among the Muslims of South Asia many are malnourished, living alongside millionaires. Millions are illiterate.[17] The pain in the lives of women is enormous.

The circumstances of women in our world are indeed diverse. Change is a shared experience. In some places the change is rapid. In others, cultural change is slow, sometimes miniscule. Women who find themselves surrounded by change but caught in the crossfire of established traditions and practices live with internal tension—and no clear resolution of it. Daily survival is the focus. Where will a woman go to find comfort and understanding, to find shepherding? Who will understand like another woman? Who is more readily available? In some situations, a woman will only have opportunity for safe interfacing with another woman. In such settings, women often instinctively comfort and help one another.

Karen Neumann and her husband, Mikel Neumann, Professor of Intercultural Studies at Western Seminary, serve as consultants to missionaries around the globe. They conclude that women are the best candidates to shepherd women across cultural lines.[18] Historically, we have witnessed the fact that sisterhood has ministered to women across cultures. Both historical and societal changes in recent years have accentuated the need for women to shepherd women. Add to that what we instinctively know and see regularly affirmed through research is the effective impact of women in evangelicalism.

According to an article on Barna Research Online, "Women Are the Backbone of the Christian Congregations in America," in "more than nine out of ten Protestant churches (and, of course 100% of Catholic churches)" in the U.S., men are in top leadership roles. "However, a new nationwide survey from the Barna Research Group suggests that women shoulder most of the responsibility for the health and vitality of the Christian faith in this country. Without women, Christianity would have nearly 60% fewer adherents."[19]

Barna's findings reflect that a greater number of women have a high degree of spiritual depth and a more significant faith commitment than men. "Women's participation levels outdistance that of men" in many areas, such as devotional time, reading the Bible, attending church, and praying. "Women are twice as likely to be involved in a discipleship process at a church [and] more often than not, take the lead role in the spiritual life of the family. Women typically emerge as the primary—or only—spiritual mentor and role model for family members. And that puts a tremendous burden on wives and mothers." Barna is "upbeat about women's emphasis on faith, [but] he [sounds] a note of caution regarding the high price women may pay for carrying excessive levels of spiritual responsibility. . . . Churches need to consider whether or not they are providing sufficient opportunities for women to receive ministry and not just provide ministry to others."

The decline Barna reports in church attendance among women who are believers coupled with what he describes as the "low levels of religious participation among women who are members of the Buster generation—those who are 34 years and under"—raises a serious question. If women are indeed the "backbone of the Christian congregations in America," why is there a noticeable weakening of the backbone? The women themselves are strong, but their involvement is weakening.

May I suggest the reason is that what women face today, given historical and societal changes, necessitates care specific to the needs of women along with relevant biblical input. Women are in new places and new roles and they're experiencing new pressures. Often time and technology work against them. They are tempted to sideline feelings. Business and too much analysis can dull their senses. "Even . . .compassion has fallen on hard times these days."[20]

Increased emotional pain has come with these societal privileges for women. It is one of the trade-offs. Women respond to this in a variety of ways. The danger is that the beauty of the female gender will be diminished rather than enhanced. Our fast-paced and troubled world can leave women emotionally needy without adequate resources on which to call. It is time to consider the directive of Titus in light of the increased emotional and spiritual needs of women. Surely these compel us to search intently for a workable solution, for a means of dispersing compassion that draws women with irresistible fervor to the Master Shepherd.

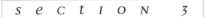

DISPERSE
compassion

people who need it

compassion comes from understanding Like-pain

meLINda's VOICE SOUNded urgent. We hurried in the heat of the summer to her home. We let ourselves in and hurried through the house to find her shut away in the darkness of her bedroom.

There she was, sitting up in her bed, holding on to her seven-and-a-half-months pregnant stomach as if someone would take him from her. *It looks like death in here, doesn't it, with all the blinds closed?* With deep emotion she began telling us that is exactly what her doctor wanted to do. Melinda had been working part-time at the hospital, but had a particularly busy week. Several times during that week she noticed that the baby was not as active as usual, but the demands of her week kept her from focusing further on what her instincts were telling her. Finally, she went to the doctor and found there was no heartbeat.

Melinda was nearly forty. This was her first pregnancy. She knew it would be her only one. She had taken expensive fertility drugs and prayed. Ever since she was a little girl all she could dream of was being a mommy. She had waited a long time . . . through two marriages.

Melinda talked continuously, repeating the same heartbreaking cry, "Please don't let them take my baby. *Please!*"

The doctor agreed that Melinda could have some time to process the loss, but she would need to be induced and go through labor to deliver their precious stillborn little boy. The next day was Mother's Day.

A small funeral followed. Then people thought she and her husband should "get on with their lives" and try to "forget this disappointment."

Melinda and Ron's pain was too deep for them to do that. They both knew the Lord personally. Their faith and service to the church had been admirable. But this was more than a speed bump. Questions no one could answer saturated their minds.

Melinda's best support came from a grief recovery group at the hospital where she worked. Melinda responded to the compassion she felt from the other women in the group who had also experienced the death of a child. They understood as no one else. They didn't say things like "You will see him again," or "God knows best." They didn't tell her everything would be OK. It was not OK, and at that point Melinda was not sure it would ever be OK. Her only biological child was no longer with her. He was in heaven, and she could not be with him. She could not hold him, feed him, cuddle him, or hear his voice. He would not blow out his first birthday candle—or any subsequent birthday candle.

Often a friend from the group would just hold her and let her cry, without feeling a need to use words. Women from the group let Melinda know it was OK—actually *good*—to cry. Sometimes they extended just a touch on the hand, a thoughtful card, or an encouraging phone message. When Melinda needed to talk, a group member just listened. She validated Melinda's incredible loss. Her son was not just tissue or a dream. He was a real little person with a heartbeat. Remembrances of his birth date memorialized his place in the family.

As weeks turned into months, Melinda and Ron began to feel that individuals from the support group extended more meaningful help than their church friends. This saddened Melinda, and soon she was able to express her needs to people in the church body. Melinda and Ron were loved by their church body. Seeing them in pain was difficult for many. Some did not know how to process it. But as Melinda and Ron began opening their lives, people began to feel an incredible compassion for them. Soon people with other losses began connecting with their feelings of loss. People wanted to understand and became proactive in expanding their understanding of such a painful loss. (Melinda and Ron never did conceive another child. Eighteen months later they adopted a precious baby girl.)

One of the things the body learned from Melinda was that she was not primarily looking for the answer to "Why." Oh, that would have been nice and she certainly asked it of God, but she realized that she might never know the answer this side of heaven. What she needed most was people who cared enough to listen to her ask the question or talk about the pain of loss, to relive those memorable seven and a half months, to be there, to love her in her loss and confusion.

Melinda gave her church a much-needed gift. She taught the body how to grieve. Oh, this didn't come easily or quickly. Initially people either ignored her at church or refused to talk about the death. She understood that people just didn't know what to say, so they said nothing. Actually the opposite was what Melinda and Ron needed most—they needed to talk about it. Each time they talked about it, they grieved a little more. This is an essential part of processing a loss.

Compassion is a powerful feeling. It drives us to extend hands of mercy even when we do not feel gifted in mercy or are not sure how to be merciful. It moves us into an arena of "Do unto others what you would have them do to you." It is a feeling of care, perhaps love. It is on the feeling level that we connect and reach out. Someone who understands like-pain is best able to move with compassion toward someone in a similar pain. The women in Melinda's grief recovery group had experienced a similar loss—miscarriage, a still-born child, the death of a baby. They had a level of understanding that enabled them to reach out in effective ways to Melinda and Ron. Once Melinda and Ron moved to a place of measured health, they were able to effectively reach out to others in their church and community with similar losses. They became catalysts in their home church for showing compassion amidst painful losses.

There is much we can learn about compassion. How do we develop compassionate hearts? How can we use the pain in our lives for good? There are eight things we learn about compassion from the story of a battered traveler in Luke 10:25–37.

the qualities of compassion

1. Compassion stops to meet needs.

A traveler was going from the big city to a smaller town seventeen miles away. The road ran through rocky, desert country. The traveler "fell into the hands of robbers. They stripped him of his clothes, beat him and went away, leaving him half dead" (Luke 10:30). When the traveler was at his worst, naked, beaten half to death, probably covered with bruises, dried blood, dirt, and sweat, a man from Samaria traveling along the same road took notice and stopped. What was his reaction to this repulsive sight? "When he saw him, he felt compassion" (10:33 NASB).

This means to be moved in the inward parts. This is a deep feeling of sympathy.[1] Webster defines *compassion* as a feeling of deep sympathy and sorrow for another who is stricken by misfortune, accompanied by a strong desire to alleviate the suffering. Synonyms are *tenderness, heart, mercy,* and *commiseration.* An antonym is *indifference.*[2]

True compassion is a heartfelt feeling that motivates one to action. The opposite is embodied in the action of the religious leaders in our story. Both clearly see the beaten traveler and both walk away *on the other side of the road,* the safe side. We do not know whether they just did not want to get involved or did not have the time since they were in a hurry to do ministry elsewhere. It is generally agreed they were going *down*, away from Jerusalem.[3] It appears they were on their way home from church. Perhaps they did not want to be late for the promised Chinese takeout or TV special that evening. We want to point the finger, but an uneasy feeling in our stomach tells us we can identify more easily than we would like with their decision to move to the safe side of the road.

In contrast, when the Samaritan saw the Jewish traveler, the Samaritan *felt compassion.* This is in striking contrast not only to the response of the priest and the Levite who passed by without stopping, but with the feelings of most Samaritans toward Jews. The long-standing animosity and prejudice would normally lead a Samaritan to express approval of such a crime perpetrated on an enemy. A Samaritan might "finish the job." At minimum he would walk away from a Jew even in a 911 roadside crisis.

Instead, we are all surprised to see the Samaritan not only stop, but respond with goodwill. The Samaritan *met the immediate physical needs* of the traveler. He recognized the needs and chose to stop and give to those needs.

Shepherding women will encompass meeting immediate physical needs. Sometimes this involves meals, transportation, and medical or child care. A member of the shepherding team may have the expertise and resources to meet these needs, or a separate Care Team may be formed to address physical needs. At minimum, we may be called upon to give of our personal time and resources in the immediate, as did the Samaritan. One who has "been there" will best understand the needs of the moment.

When Lily's husband died, her widowed friend Sally was there with a hug. Telephone calls were made, first to 911, then immediate family and friends. Within hours dinner was prepared for extended family coming into town that evening. A funeral home was secured and appointments made. Sally seemed to know just what to do during those first hours of confusion and shock. Why? Sally had "been there." She knew well the feelings and the immediate physical need for a hug, phone calls, food, and other arrangements.

2. Compassion costs—but it reflects God's heart.

What did it cost the Samaritan to help the traveler? He probably had to rearrange the nicely packed suitcase to find cloths, oil, and wine. The time and energy called for would surely cause a major delay in his business trip. The money required would certainly mean hamburgers instead of steak the rest of the way. Since time is money and both are in short demand, the Samaritan made a costly decision—but then so did Jesus. Jesus and the Samaritan reflect the heart of God. Extended care to another is costly, but has this not always been God's heart for His people? Loving God and others is the greatest commandment. It is the summation of all the others.

The Scripture doesn't give a time line, except to say that "the next day" he left two silver coins to pay for the traveler's care. It seems clear that the Samaritan spent the rest of the first day—the evening—with the traveler. Wouldn't you love to be a fly on the wall? I suspect if the traveler was conscious at all, the Samaritan had opportunity to express sympathy, to enter into the traveler's *emotional needs*. The traveler's plans were interrupted. His trip may have been business, and the profits from an important business deal could have been stolen. At any rate, he faced grieving over the loss of whatever he had set out to accomplish and a feeling of injustice and violation at being robbed. And we are not told how this Jewish traveler felt about receiving care from a Samaritan!

Certainly shepherding others will require time and resources. Since there are only twenty-four hours in a day, it means giving precious hours to another. If our life purpose is serving our Lord, certainly our time has already been committed—to Him. Those hours unexpectedly given to another were in a sense already earmarked for service. Perhaps more thought could be given to built-in margins for service and simpler budgeted lifestyles, resulting in intentional surplus for others. One of the amazing things about serving God is that in giving away, we often gain the most!

3. Compassion is not limited by its object but by its subject.

The quality and extent of compassion lies in the control of its subject. The Samaritan made a choice to love. He did not evaluate the worthiness of the traveler to receive his love. Like the Samaritan, we need to see the *absolute value* of others, a value that is inherent as image bearers. We are grateful that the Samaritan did not base his decision to extend care based on the *relative value*, the value of what the traveler could do for him.

As image bearers we share the likeness of God. David expressed wonderment at this fact:

> *What is man that you are mindful of him,*
> *and the son of man that you care for him?*
> *Yet you have made him a little lower than the heavenly beings*
> *and crowned him with glory and honor.*
> *You have given him dominion over the works of your hands;*
> *you have put all things under his feet.*
> (Psalm 8:4–6 NLT)

Every human being is created in the image of God, not just those who respond to His invitation for salvation. The extent of our compassion will greatly increase as we see the absolute value of others. If we shepherd others based on what others can do for us, not only will our ministry be frustrating, but we will miss many opportunities to touch the heart of another, to extend Christ's hands and feet to a needy world.

4. Compassionate community provides recovery.

The inn was a needed place of recovery, a place of community. People need a safe place for full recovery, and not one of us alone can provide all that people need to recover from a crisis. It often takes a community to provide health. The Samaritan recognized this. It was a healthy decision on his part. The two silver coins were two days' wages—quite a loss to a businessman—but provided two months' care at the inn.[4] The Samaritan had the monetary resources, while others at the inn had the medical and (hopefully) emotional resources to bring healing.

This is a critical aspect of shepherding! It takes a village, a community, or a church body! More effective ministry is provided by teams. One person rarely has sufficient resources, but even so, the body was designed to work in tandem. As an orchestra plays in harmony to produce a pleasing sound, so many parts of the body work together "for the common good" (1 Corinthians 12:7). Members using identified spiritual gifts, talents, and experience supply all the needed elements for restoration.

5. Compassion need not enmesh.

The Samaritan's own plans and purposes were not trashed in view of helping another. He did continue his trip. He did not become enmeshed. Physical and emotional boundaries were maintained. The Samaritan did not forsake what God had called him to. Neither did he abandon the needy traveler because of his own life's goals.

Again, the contributions of a team enable one person to maintain healthy boundaries and maintain personal goals while caring for another. Understandably, there will be times when one takes a "time out" to minister more fully to a given need. But this decision should be intentional and with God's direction, rather than by default. Attitudes are powerfully affected by these factors. A choice to stop and give aid results in a sense of fulfillment in helping another human. Conversely when one is coerced or pressured by guilt, the ministry may soon become drudgery. Caring for others can be difficult and trying and it can cost a great deal emotionally and physically, but attitude may directly increase or decrease the caregiver's energy flow.

6. Compassion looks beyond differences.

How was the Samaritan different from the traveling Jew? The Jews viewed the Samaritans as "half-breeds" both physically and spiritually. The Samaritans were a mixed-blood race resulting from the intermarriage of Israelites left behind when the people of the northern kingdom were exiled and Gentiles brought into the land by the

Assyrians (2 Kings 17:24). Bitter hostility existed between Jews and Samaritans in Jesus' day.

The Jews and Samaritans disagreed on the place of worship. The question the woman at the well asked in John 4 was a very intelligent question—a long-debated issue between the Samaritans and the Jews: "Our fathers worshiped on this mountain, but you Jews claim that the place where we must worship is in Jerusalem" (v. 20). The Samaritans believed that Mt. Gerizim rather than Mt. Ebal was the mountain on which Moses had commanded an altar to be built (Deuteronomy 27:4–6). The Samaritans built a temple on Mt. Gerizim in 400 B.C., which the Jews destroyed in 128. Both actions increased hostility between the two groups.[5]

There were racial and cultural differences, as well. Deep prejudices existed because of them. Those differences were not excluded from the parable. They were a powerful backdrop to the story. They accentuated the point that although compassion may acknowledge differences, it looks beyond differences to extend care.

7. Compassion results from understanding like-pain.

Though there were many differences, there was one all-important similarity—they had experienced similar pain. This is the most powerful dynamic of the story. *The Samaritan had compassion, because he too was a victim, a person in a situation over which he had no control.* He understood. He too had been treated unjustly. The traveler was a victim of robbery. The Samaritan had been victimized his entire life. But he didn't let victimization eat him alive or make him bitter. He didn't enter into the prejudicial actions all around him, those his culture dictated. Instead, he turned the bitter past into good. He used his painful past experiences for good. He "had mercy on him" (Luke 7:37). Perhaps feelings of the past surfaced when the Samaritan saw the traveler victimized and "left for dead" through no choice of his own.

No one quite understands like a person with similar pain in his or her experience. Similar pain brings a greater depth of understanding. Compassion flourishes in a garden of understanding.

Understanding gained from personal experience or from a friend or family member's experience fosters compassion.

I would like to think when the Samaritan returned, which he promised to do, that a lifelong friendship followed. After all, not only had he saved the traveler's life, he had something basic in common with this robbery victim.

8. Compassion flows from the forgiver and the forgiven.

Although the Samaritan's place in life was different from the traveler's, the Samaritan could extend mercy and grace. Why? There is only one way. Although the parable doesn't go into this kind of detail, in reality the Samaritan's actions reveal one who is able to forgive others for their prejudice and abusive behavior. Often it is out of our own pain and poverty that we give the most meaningful expressions of love. *Those who have received compassion and love give it more easily.* Jesus' words ring true: "He who has been forgiven little loves little" (Luke 7:47).

We are all victims of sin, of the abuse of this world in some form. Aren't you grateful for those who have been Jesus' hands and feet to you? For those who have extended His love and compassion when you were the least lovely?

Remember the context of this parable. Jesus does not directly answer the expert-in-the-law's question "Who is my neighbor?" Rather, He changes the emphasis of the question. He asked, "Are you a neighbor?" Although three men came into the traveler's neighborhood, only the Samaritan was a neighbor. In essence, Jesus says that if you really love God you will love others. You will find your neighbor in the person at whom you otherwise would not look. In being neighborly you will find your neighbor in the person who needs help.[6]

Extending acts of kindness is a choice. Feelings of compassion certainly can come from understanding like-pain, if we choose to process our pain in a healthy way. When pain turns to bitterness and rejection, we quench the Spirit of God and lose feelings of compassion for others in similar situations.

All of us can relate to some kind of loss in life. In our loss of a good grade, of a possession, of a job, of a dream, of a relationship, we relate in some measure to Melinda's loss. But the full depth of losing a child—your only pregnancy, one you have dreamed of all your life—can only be felt by Melinda. Other women with similar experiences can come closer than those who have not had a like-experience, but no one feels *exactly* what another feels. The personality, experiences, and family makeup of each individual are too unique to assume that we fully share another's precise feelings. Even a husband and wife process losses differently, which often leads to a misunderstanding of each other's grieving. This is often the reason for conflict and divorce among couples who have lost a child to death or permanent handicap.

Melinda's willingness to share her experience with her church increased compassion by opening the door to understanding. Like the "Good Samaritan," she chose to use her pain for good.

a reflection of compassion

Agnes Gonxha Bjoaxhiu (1910–1997), better known as Mother Teresa, has left us with images of compassion in action. Although Protestantism disagrees theologically with Catholicism, we would do well to take a closer look at a level of compassion that has impacted the world. If you want to stir your own heart or the hearts of people around you, spend an hour watching love in action in *Mother Teresa* and the many women who carry on the work around the world that Mother Teresa began on the streets of Calcutta.[7] Today there are thousands of women in 126 nations operating more than five hundred homes and clinics dispensing compassion.[8] These women see each person as a life created in the image of God to be treated with respect and with dignity. These women choose a lifetime of poverty to more effectively disperse compassion to the discarded.

What would lead a woman to extend this kind of compassion to the "poorest of the poor"? Mother Teresa came from a wealthy home in Albania. Her mother came from a wealthy home and her father was a successful businessman. When she and her two siblings were young, her father died, leaving her family in poverty. Her mother embroidered and sold cloth to earn a living. She was also religious and generous toward the needy. Mother Teresa knew the struggles of poverty. But her mother influenced her to think of others, to pray for provision, and live with little materially. At the age of eighteen, Mother Teresa felt the call of God and so left home at the cost of never seeing her mother or sister again.[9] Mother Teresa understood wealth and she understood poverty.

After ten years of study, then seventeen years of teaching geography to middle-class girls in Calcutta, she heard the "call within a call" to leave teaching and move to the streets of Calcutta. This sacrifice was "the most difficult thing I have ever done. It was more difficult than to leave my family and my country."[10] She paid the price and went.

> Whether ministering to lepers knocking at the order's door, a dying man lying in a gutter, or unwanted babies, sparing them from abortion and ministering to the mothers, Mother Teresa and the more than four thousand sisters of the Missionaries of Charity dispensed their loving acts. *They did this by compassionately identifying with those they helped.* . . . Mother Teresa was recognized world wide as the very personification of compassion.[11]

Although Mother Teresa received countless honors, her response was the same, "I am nothing. God is all."[12] This is the bedrock of those who disperse compassion as a lifestyle. *A life of compassion often has its roots in understanding like-pain.* Underneath that understanding is the desire to know God's heart, and in knowing to reflect His unconditional love, even to those who could not love in return. A lifestyle of compassion is the reflection of living a life in full-faced focus on God.

people who need compassion

The Bible tells us that our Good Shepherd "had compassion" toward the people in need around Him (Matthew 9:36; 14:14; 15:32; 20:34). "When he saw the crowds, he had *compassion* on them because they were harassed and helpless, like sheep without a shepherd" (Matthew 9:36, italics added). To be harassed is to be bullied and oppressed,[13] to be faint, to grow weary of body and soul in the strife against sin. To be helpless is to be cast down or cast out, to be unable to rescue oneself or escape one's tormentors.[14]

Shepherd and author Phillip Keller enlightens our understanding of a helpless sheep. The condition of a "cast" sheep clearly shows how Jesus saw this crowd of people. Sometimes a sheep lies down in a depression in the ground and rolls on its side to stretch out or relax. That causes the center of gravity to change so that her feet can no longer touch the ground. In a panic, the sheep actually works her way deeper into the depression in the ground. Gases soon build up in the rumen, expand, and cut off blood circulation to the extremities of the body. Now the cast sheep is helpless, lying on her back with her feet in the air, frantically struggling to stand up. Sometimes she will bleat, but generally she lashes about in frightened frustration.

If the shepherd does not arrive within a short period of time to set her on her feet again, she will die. A hot sun will hasten death. This is one reason a shepherd must continually watch his sheep. If the shepherd is gone for a day or more ("sheep without a shepherd") the frantic sheep will surely die. A cast sheep is also vulnerable to attack. Buzzards, dogs, coyotes, and cougars all know a cast sheep is easy prey and that death is not far away. This is an ever-present danger for sheep, a major concern for shepherds. Once a shepherd notices that a sheep is missing, he is quick to run and find her, knowing every minute matters.[15]

Jesus understood that people are often like cast sheep. Often life-circumstances and our reaction to them take us to a place where we lose our equilibrium and find ourselves immobile emotionally and at times physically. We "grow weary of body and soul in strife against sin," and often we are not able to rescue ourselves or escape our perpetrators. They know we are easy prey. The enemy prowls around like a lion, looking for someone to devour. Jesus healed and taught those who were "harassed and helpless." He expressed His feelings of tenderness and mercy through action.

Melinda and Ron found themselves "cast down," unable to restore equilibrium by themselves. We have all found ourselves in such a place. We have need for a compassionate shepherd.

The picture of the shepherd restoring a cast sheep reveals an intimate tenderness, like our Good Shepherd. Once the shepherd finds the cast sheep, he gently rolls her over on her side, relieving the pressure of gases in the rumen. Then he tenderly rubs her limbs, restoring the circulation, and speaks words of correction and compassion. Little by little the sheep gains her equilibrium. Starts to walk, though stumbling at first; soon she joins the rest of the flock.[16]

Jesus saw people as cast sheep without a shepherd, threatening sure death emotionally, spiritually, and physically. Compassion moved Him to action, a critical message of the parable of the battered traveler.

The story is told of a Special Olympics race that started out well. But soon one little boy stumbled on the asphalt, tumbled over a couple of times, and began to cry. The other eight turned around and went back—every one of them. One girl with Down Syndrome bent down and kissed him and said, "This will make it better." Then all nine racers linked arms and walked together to the finish line.

An Internet source says of this story: "Deep down we know this one thing: what matters in this life is more than winning for ourselves. What matters is helping others win, even if it means slowing down and changing our course."[17] The man from Samaria slowed down and changed his course. So did our Master Shepherd. And so should we.

the master shepherd met women at their point of pain

"mom! I've lost the baby!"

Andrea could barely get the words out. Once Mom arrived she would find the unbelievable, the incomprehensible. A little plastic zip-lock bag with what looked like—but could it really be?—a tiny leg with toes and an arm with fingers. Andrea's pain was compounded further when she was asked to sign a form at the hospital calling it an "involuntary abortion."

This would be Andrea's third heartbreaking attempt to have a much-wanted child. It would be her third miscarriage at twelve weeks. Unlike the previous miscarriages, this time she had something tangible to look at, to help memorialize a family member she and her husband would not have the privilege of raising. They would bury the precious evidence under a rose bush named in the baby's honor.

Although others were quick to reassure them the baby could not be in a better place—in heaven—and that they were still young and could "try again," they were not comforted. Everything in a woman's body gears up for the development and delivery of a baby. Suddenly this comes to an abrupt halt as the body, for some unknown reason, dispels the fetus. The woman feels acute pain physically, emotionally, mentally, and spiritually. A new little person, a new part of her family, someone with whom she has already bonded and whom she greatly loves, is now gone.

Andrea felt abandoned. She was angry with God. Her husband seemed to "move on" while she couldn't even accomplish the basic tasks in her day. She believed he didn't love the baby as much as she. She couldn't have a big memorial service and invite all her friends to tell how they knew her child, to share their good memories. Her own memories were precious few. She felt alone in her grief. She didn't feel that anyone really understood. She was devastated.

No one seemed to understand—with one exception. Michelle was there the day after. She dropped in for a few minutes with flowers and a hug. She called a couple of days later and said she was praying and that she cared. A card in the mail, a voice mail message, and then a longer visit. Michelle listened. Michelle was comfortable with Andrea's tears, with her pain, and even with her anger. Andrea soon learned that Michelle understood because she too had experienced the pain of miscarriage. She knew that part of that pain never goes away. Special holidays, birthdays, and other same-aged children would always remind the mother of a family member who was missing at the dinner table.

Andrea did not need to pretend with Michelle. She could be real. Michelle's messages right from the start met Andrea at her point of pain. Michelle understood how difficult it is to grieve for someone you cannot see. Michelle understood how a mother knows her unborn child in a way no one else can. She understood that the pain needed to be acknowledged and processed. She wanted to see Andrea move to a place of peace despite the pain. This would take time, she realized, and Andrea would get there at her own pace—but she would get there. It gave Andrea hope to see Michelle after multiple miscarriages in a place of peace.

Meeting women at their point of pain is inherent in dispensing true compassion. People who need compassion most are those in emotional, physical, mental, or spiritual pain. Jesus is a wonderful example of One who met women at their point of pain, their point of need.

Studying three women in the New Testament will highlight how the Master Shepherd cared for women. Perhaps you will want to study these and other examples in the Bible by asking three questions:

1. What was the woman's greatest source of pain at the time of her encounter with Jesus?
2. Did Jesus recognize her pain?
3. What issue did Jesus address first, and how did He address it?

"Liz taylor" of samaria
John 4:2–42

Traditionally known as the Woman at the Well, "Liz" first encounters Jesus at the well in the heat of noonday. He is tired and thirsty. His opening question is task-orientated: "Will you give me a drink?"

Liz's first words to Jesus follow a predictable pattern of gender communication. Her focus is on relationship. "You are a Jew and I am a Samaritan woman. How can you ask me for a drink?" Don't you understand that Jews and Samaritans do not associate with each other, and that Jewish men and women don't normally speak to each other in public? Certainly a Jewish rabbi would never have initiated a public conversation with a woman nor even suggested drinking water from a Samaritan's cup. This is not politically correct!

What was this woman's greatest source of pain? Did Jesus recognize her pain? How did He address it?

Jesus knew that relationships were important to Liz. He also knew that she was in a lot of pain because of five broken relationships in the past and a current sixth precarious one. He knew that she had a hole in her soul and was trying to fill it with men. He knew why she came alone to the well at noon, rather than with other women in the evening. The pain of broken relationships made her an outcast among other women. Liz was well known in her village but not respected or loved as she longed to be.

Jesus' conversation with her gave her value, something she did not receive from the men who had discarded her. In Jewish law a man could divorce his wife if she became "displeasing" to him (Deuteronomy 24:1). The Jews held that a woman might be divorced twice or at the most three times. Only the husband could issue a certificate of divorce. The wife had no real recourse.

If Samaritan law was similar, then this woman, the "Liz Taylor of Samaria," not only felt the rejection of relationship after relationship but was marginalized socially. Perhaps the reason she was not married to the man she was now living with was that she had reached her limit of legal divorces. We don't know. We do know that she knew what it was to feel rejected and devalued. Jesus met her at her point of pain. He expressed value in her personhood by speaking to her in public.

Jesus further valued her intellect. He took her questions seriously. They were not diversions. What they were discussing was the religious issue that separated the Samaritans and the Jews! If the woman's questions were a diversion from the intended conversation, certainly Jesus would have diverted back to the topic at hand. No! This was the topic at hand! Once the woman's understanding of who Jesus was unfolded—notice the progression of her understanding: a Jew; one greater than our father Jacob; a prophet; the Messiah—she would have realized, *Here is a man who can answer this age-old question! No one else seems to be able to resolve it. Who is right, the Jews or the Samaritans?* Her response revealed her own understanding: "I know that Messiah (called Christ) is coming. When he comes, he will explain everything to us."

Jesus expressed value to this non-Jewish woman by revealing His identity as the Messiah. This was the only occasion before His trial when Jesus specifically stated that He was the Messiah.[1] And He revealed this to a woman, a woman who had been repeatedly devalued by men.

Jesus expressed value to Liz by wrapping His response to her acknowledged marital pain in affirming words. Twice He noted that she was truthful, she was right. Words of condemnation were noticeably absent. Jesus did not minimize truth; rather, He communicated truth in a way that conveyed respect for her as an image bearer.

Later, in her excitement Liz left her water jug and hurried back to her village to declare, "Come, see a man who told me everything I ever did. Could this be the Christ?" Did Jesus *really* tell her *everything* she ever did? In the few verses recorded we read little of her biography. However, the Chief Shepherd's interaction with her reveals much about her life. Liz's entire life was characterized by a deep need to be valued, to be loved. She had tried many things, many relationships. Nothing had worked. Each discarded relationship only increased her emptiness and magnified her pain. Jesus was the first to recognize that pain, identify her greatest need, and fill it with "living water." The motivation of her life, of everything she ever did, was to end the intense pain of needing to be valued, to be truly loved. Not used, then trashed. But forgiven and loved unconditionally simply for who she was.

Liz Taylor of Samaria became Liz the Evangelist of Samaria. Who would believe a story like this? *Many* in Samaria did!

Jesus' example of meeting Liz at her greatest point of pain is one those who are shepherds of women should follow. This will be natural for many women, for most women do have the ability to enter into the feelings of others, especially if like-experiences are shared. Ignoring a woman's point of pain while giving instruction is less effective. If Jesus had lectured Liz, what a different result might have taken place. Instead, He dispensed truth sensitively, with perfect timing in the context of her pain.

A shepherd of women may be the first person who expresses

value to the Liz Taylors in her community. Although Liz wasn't politically correct or even socially adept, she was created in the image of God and needed living water. Women have an all-encompassing need for loving relationships. They were created with that need. Jesus is the only One who can meet those deep longings for intimacy. The body of Christ was His plan for community, even for the Liz Taylors of our cities.

the CHRONICaLLy iLL "mystery womaN"
Matthew 9:20–22; Mark 5:25–34; Luke 8:43–48

A second example of the Master Shepherd meeting a woman at her point of pain is repeated in three of the Gospels. We almost miss this woman in pain. She is hidden in the middle of a huge crowd pressing around Jesus and Jairus, the ruler of the synagogue. They are on their way to see Jairus's dying daughter. Jairus was a spiritual and community leader, someone of great renown in the community. Many were interested in following Jesus and Jairus. But somewhere in that crowd was a woman who wanted to remain anonymous.

"A woman who was there" is how we are introduced to her in Mark 5:25. As we follow the action words in verses 26–28 we see her story unfold. She

- *suffered* a great deal under the care of many doctors,
- *spent all* she had,
- *grew worse* instead of getting better,
- *heard* about Jesus,
- *came up behind* Him in the crowd,
- *touched* His cloak because she
- *thought*, "If I just touch his clothes, *I will be healed.*"

This Mystery Woman was generally shunned. Anyone touching her or touching anything she touched would be made ceremonially unclean (Leviticus 15:19–23, 25–33). It would be unusual to see her in public. More than likely because of her condition she was not married. She probably had few friends. The cost of medical care and protection left her in poverty.

She must have grown physically weak and pale after twelve years of bleeding, to say nothing of the odor. It was likely that her hemorrhaging was not a blood-clotting problem, or she would have bled to death. "Bleeding between periods is more frequently associated with a malignancy than is heavy bleeding at the time of the period."[2] Whether the bleeding was monthly or daily, we are not told. Assuredly she was isolated, avoided, and excluded. She could not go into the temple or a synagogue for corporate worship—not for the last twelve years! She would be hesitant to join the women shopping in the streets for fruits and vegetables. People may have assumed God was punishing her for a secret sin. No wonder she was a Mystery Woman. Who would know her? Who would want to know her? It was much safer to remain anonymous.

What was this woman's greatest source of pain? Did Jesus recognize her pain? How did He address it?

As this chronically ill Mystery Woman had hoped, touching the edge of Jesus' clothes stopped the twelve-year-long flow of blood from her body. If the story ended here we could say that Jesus met her at her point of pain: He healed her body. But Jesus knew her greatest point of pain was not her physical illness. It was the damage to her soul, to her personhood, that twelve years of isolation had brought about. When Jesus "realized that power had gone out from him," He stopped the ruler of the synagogue in the middle of his hurried walk to his dying daughter. He stopped the large crowd that followed them. The Mystery Woman was important enough for Him to ask a seemingly ridiculous question: "Who touched me?" The crowd waited. Seconds turned into minutes. Everyone was touching everyone else; the crowd "pressed" around Jesus. What kind of answer was Jesus looking for?

While everyone waited, this anonymous woman calculated the risk of losing her anonymity. She hoped Jesus would withdraw the question and move on. Yet she knew Jesus had healed her. She was sure of that. But she was filled with fear at the thought of everyone focusing on her. She did not know what Jesus' reaction to her might be. Would she be pronounced unclean again? Would she be punished for touching Jesus?

The Mystery Woman was afraid. "Then the woman, seeing that she could not go unnoticed" (she had tried!) "came trembling and fell at his feet" (Luke 8:47). In the presence of this huge crowd, and Jairus himself, the woman gave her testimony, probably the first time publicly! She told what led her to dare to touch Jesus' garment. She declared that in touching, she had been instantly healed.

Jesus met this chronically ill woman at her point of greatest need. The shame and marginalization she had lived with for twelve years were wiped away when Jesus publicly declared, "Daughter, your faith has healed you. Go in peace and be freed from your suffering" (Mark 5:34).

Jesus commended her for her faith. Jesus saw more than a contaminating chronically ill body. He repaired a self-concept that could have kept her isolated and crippled the rest of her life, a shame that would have been more contaminating than her physical illness. He commended her for her faith, knowing the courage it took to pursue Him in the crowd. He publicly affirmed her and introduced a new woman. Jesus *clarified*. Her faith in Him *healed* her. She was a woman of faith *before* she was healed. *After* she was healed she took ownership of her true identity. She was no longer mysterious or anonymous.

This is the only time in the New Testament that Jesus calls a woman "daughter." Daughter is a term used in family relationships. Jesus is calling her out of isolation into a relationship with Him. No one is anonymous to Jesus. He meets women at their point of pain. Faith is always required. Jesus honored her faith.

Often women exhibit a pressing felt need, but underlying that felt need is a real need. Any chronic condition will redefine a woman. Shepherds may need to examine a woman's long-held definition of herself and determine its similarity to the biblical definition of woman, a daughter of the King! Perhaps a shepherd's greatest contribution will be ministering to the real need, the soul need. Like Jesus, the place the shepherd should begin is at the point of the woman's pain.

"monica" of jerusalem

Our last example of the Master Shepherd meeting a woman at her point of pain is found in John 8:1–11. John gives us a brief account of "Monica," better known as "the woman taken in adultery."

The religious leaders clearly arranged a setup. They force the woman "caught in adultery" to stand in the temple courts so that they can press a point of law. "In the Law Moses commanded us to stone such women. Now what do you say?" they ask. They continue to press Jesus for an answer. It is obvious that Monica is not their main concern. Her personhood is invisible to them.

Jesus did not respond to them immediately. He "bent down and started to write on the ground with his finger." If this scene were filmed today, the camera would zoom in on Jesus' finger as He wrote on the ground, the voices of the leaders continuing to clamor in the background.

Then He stood up and said to them, "If any one of you is without sin, let him be the first to throw a stone at her." Our camera doesn't get close enough to read what Jesus wrote; we only know that the combination of His words and His letters sent a message that quieted the demands of the leaders and left only Jesus and the woman standing in the courtyard.

What was this woman's greatest source of pain? Did Jesus recognize her pain? How did He address it?

Jesus' first words to her addressed her pain: "Woman, where are they? Has no one condemned you?" Condemnation certainly was the intent of the religious leaders. The Law said she should be stoned, and they were pressing the charge. Jesus' message to the leaders must have stung them. Their response was to walk away; repentance is not recorded.

Jesus' words to Monica were compassionate: "Then neither do I condemn you. Go now and leave your life of sin." Jesus did not diminish the truth. But neither did He condemn her personhood. He valued her as a woman. He spoke with respect and grace. Her greatest source of pain was the condemnation she felt. The man involved in the presumed act of adultery was neither present nor included in the discussion. Jesus met this woman at her point of pain, removed the emotional shame, and charged her to live a new life of freedom in Christ.

Condemnation or shrapnel from condemnation is epidemic in some religious circles. The response of shepherds of women is key to healing. Certainly sin is sin, and we need to have the same perspective as the Scriptures, make no mistake about it. In the same way our Master Shepherd approached women in pain, so shepherds should lift the weight of shame so that women can see new light, new life in Christ. Women who receive genuine Spirit-filled compassion can hardly miss the message of value, of unconditional love that the gospel embodies.

In each of the New Testament stories we have talked about in this chapter, Liz, the Mystery Woman, and Monica all responded to the gentle yet truthful approach of Jesus. They felt His acceptance and His valuing them. In each case, this opened the door for emotional and spiritual healing. Can you imagine "the rest of the story" in each of these women's lives? Can you see Liz going from town to town to tell her story—it is just too good to keep in one small community! Perhaps several new converts join her, and together the gospel is given. For the first time she feels loved and is able to walk the path of establishing healthy relationships.

The Mystery Woman becomes well known, as she too cannot keep her story a secret. She loves telling her story. She loves even more the fact that others come near. She has moved from isolation into a warm, fulfilling place of relationships—perhaps like old times, before her illness. Through her relationships, others come to know this One who changed her life forever.

I suspect that dear Monica, forgiven and renewed in her desire to follow this Jesus, may have made a conscious decision for purity. After all, Jesus may have saved her from being stoned, from physical death. That is what the religious leaders were advocating. A new reputation and a new life may have followed our John 8 account. Perhaps this "woman caught in adultery" should be given a new name to fit a new identity. Perhaps Monica would be better identified as one "touched by an angel." Just as the Lord does not freeze-frame any segment of our lives and hang it in a gallery for all to see, neither should we. Instead, a video may be more appropriate, a moving frame that captures her ongoing maturity.

Shepherds, by extending compassion to those who need it most, may be able to open the door to forgiveness, healing, and the truth of who Jesus is. Compassion may bring in the sunshine of a new identity as a daughter of the King!

storytelling

The woman at the well in John 4 and the woman healed from chronic illness in Mark 5 both told their stories to Jesus. It is in the telling that we discover more about their inner lives. We discover the source of pain. In the opening story of this chapter, Michelle's miscarriage experiences were a great encouragement to Andrea in the midst of her own painful miscarriage. How does storytelling fit into dispensing compassion?

There are several reasons that listening to others tell their stories is important. Jesus knew that storytelling is an important communication tool for both men and women. "Storytelling, particularly in context of a pastoral care relationship, becomes a sacrament, revealing God's presence in the midst of tragedy."[3]

1. Stories connect people.

Stories create community. It is in sharing experiences that we write history with another person. It is in the telling of those shared experiences that we develop commonalities and friendships. We create emotional ties, we deepen relationships. We look for common experiences and relate on those levels.

2. Stories define who we are.

Stories define what is important to us and redefine us in new situations. As we mature, our stories become more truthful and we become more authentic and consistent in the telling. Listening to other's stories reveals much about how they see themselves and their life experiences. "Feeling" words and a woman's perceptions give great insight into her soul. How does this woman define herself? How do others define her? Was the woman in John 8 always defined as "the woman taken in adultery"? Or will "the rest of the story" move her community past the freeze-frame of adultery to her new life in Christ? Will she accept forgiveness? Will she redefine herself as a woman of integrity and purity? Listening to her story will reveal the answer.

3. Stories help make sense of our experiences.

We came into this world as part of someone else's story. Whether we began as a twinkle in someone's eye or an unplanned physical act, we contributed to their story and we began a new story. Stories help explain our experiences, help us to laugh, and give meaning. Placing our stories side by side, like building blocks, gives form to our lives. The stories of our parents and grandparents provide an essential backdrop to our story. Our past helps us make sense of our present, which may empower us to choose a better future.

Others' stories help us not feel alone in ours. Their insights give us a better understanding of our story. Michelle's story certainly helped Andrea make sense of her own painful miscarriage experiences. It helped her move forward despite the pain. "A significant element of ministry is to remind ourselves and others of how important it is to pay attention to what is happening to us. The events of yesteryear, even yesterday, are part of a drama called ourselves."[4]

4. Stories are theological autobiographies.

Stories tell how the Word became flesh in me. They tell of God's presence in the tragedies and celebrations of life. Jesus used plenty of stories. It is primarily stories that are recorded in the Gospels. If Jesus exegeted books of the Old Testament, those priceless sermons have not been preserved for us. Rather, it is the stories that have been kept and passed down from generation to generation. Jesus told stories like the parable we often call "The Good Samaritan," to illustrate what loving our neighbor really looks like. We see Jesus doing the same thing the Samaritan did. We come to know the compassionate love of our Lord through this story.

The gospel of Jesus Christ is heard through our story. We are only a chapter in God's big story—the novel of eternity—but a very important chapter! Realizing we are only one chapter puts our life in perspective. When we focus on the short story of Deborah or Esther, we have the advantage of placing their lives into the bigger picture of God's plan for His people. The rest of the book has not been written yet, so we are not able to see future chapters and know how our life fits into the future. But we do have the advantage of the past and can see that God's plan is *big*. Perhaps seeing the part one life plays will give hope and meaning to tragedy and pain and the courage to move through.

5. Stories give hope.

As Michelle listened to Andrea's story, she had the power to accept and affirm Andrea and God's presence in her life. This gave Andrea powerful hope. When Andrea heard how Michelle redefined herself as a mother of four, with two living children, this gave her hope. Reading biblical stories of characters who endured tragedy and pain not only gives us hope, but gives us the perspective and courage to "keep going." Hope enables us to move our focus from the pain and to the Lord. This positions us to receive from Him all we need to learn and grow in the pain.

6. Each story is a gift, a treasure to the world.

No two stories are exactly alike—not yours, not the stories you will hear. What a reflection of our amazing God! That is why each story is so important. Each chapter of God's big story was ordained to be written. It is an integral part of the novel of His grace! "Who I am is the only one of me in the universe. This unique story is the finest gift I have. If I do not narrate it, it will remain silent. . . . By digging it out and sharing it, it becomes a sacred treasure, a gift for use in renewing the lives of all who touch it."[5]

7. Valuing a woman's story is valuing the woman.

Listening to a woman's story gives powerful insight into her feelings and thoughts. Her story reveals how she makes sense of her life, how she defines herself, and how she perceives God's involvement. Michelle's ability to listen and value Andrea's story helped Andrea understand the pain and process it in a healthy way. Andrea slowly began to redefine herself and her life after the miscarriages because Michelle was willing to listen.

Shepherds of women clearly dispense compassion to women who need it most by following Jesus' example of meeting women at their point of pain. Listening intently to each story as if you were searching for diamonds in the rough conveys value to women and opens understanding to women in pain.

Listening to women's stories is one important aspect of good shepherding. A diversity of skills is needed to effectively listen. The last segment of this book focuses on that fourth aspect of shepherding a woman's heart: *diversity of skills.* We begin with the profile of a good shepherd in contrast to the pain of poor shepherding.

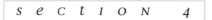

DIVERSIFY
SKILLS

people who give it

profile of a
good shepherd

as a young woman Sandy felt drawn to God. When a neighbor befriended Sandy and drew her into a religious circle, Sandy eagerly followed. Ten years later, once Sandy and her husband were fully involved in this group, Sandy began to question some of the group's beliefs. Immediately it became clear that questioning was not allowed. Those who raised questions were labeled "apostate" and reported. No one was permitted to raise questions even with family members at home. Each member was under obligation to report any violation. Sandy became frightened as leaders watched her more closely and questioned her every move. Sandy knew she needed to leave the group. Little did she realize that years of harassment and threat would follow her family's leaving this religious organization.

Initially, Sandy did not want to be involved in another religious group. Understandably, she was afraid of repeating her painful experience. She was confused. She simply wanted to know God. Why had she followed this path that led to such bondage and fear? She had trusted her leaders. Now she felt betrayed and used. Sandy felt the leaders cared about her only as she advanced their cause. They were not there to care for her and her family. Their agenda was destructive.[1]

POOR SHEPHERDING

The Bible validates the pain of poor shepherding. In Ezekiel 34:3–4 the sovereign Lord charged that the shepherds of Israel ruled the people "harshly and brutally" because they cared only about the "choice animals." Their motivation for focusing on the choice animals was selfish. They enjoyed the curds and wool clothing these animals supplied. They cared for themselves rather than the flock. Their agenda was destructive. The Lord's accusation against Israel's shepherds was severe:

> *Woe to the shepherds of Israel who only take care of themselves! Should not shepherds take care of the flock? . . . You have not strengthened the weak or healed the sick or bound up the injured. You have not brought back the strays or searched for the lost. (Ezekiel 34:2, 4)*

How did this poor shepherding impact the flock? The sheep were "scattered because there was no shepherd" to look for them or to care for them. As a result, the sheep "became food for all the wild animals" (v. 5). Often women in pain have "scattered" and become "food for the wild animals" because there was no one to shepherd them. Pain is an open door for the Enemy. It is a time of great vulnerability. It is a time when shepherding is most critical. Women who are willing to go beyond caring for "choice animals" are so needed!

But most of us in the body of Christ naturally gravitate to the healthy because, like the shepherds in Israel, we receive something for our efforts. Women completing a weekly Bible study program usually affirm their leaders and the Bible study experience as the study comes to a close. They have the good feelings of completion. There is a beginning and an end to the program, and the end marks productivity. In the process, the women learn something more about the Bible and themselves. They believe their efforts were well spent and feel rewarded. Success is measurable.

Bible study is certainly gratifying and essential. And, yes, healthy sheep *do* need good food and a safe environment in which to grow. Even the choice animals need shepherding. But often our ministries to women are only ministries to the *healthy*. How many ministries, groups, or programs do you have in your ministry to women that focus specifically on the injured or the lost? This kind of shepherding is often messy, and months later there may be few visible signs of fruit. Sometimes the lost sheep repel our search-and-rescue efforts and are open season for hunters of all species. Often it is difficult to measure our productivity or celebrate success. Delayed gratification is difficult to embrace.

Similarly, the young—whether in physical or in spiritual years— are many times not a primary focus in our planning. While their youthful energy is admired, other facets of their lives are foreign to older women. The impulse is to influence them to live life in the comfort zone of the previous generation, rather than gleaning valuable perspective from a present generation. We invite them to join *us*, rarely taking initiative to visit *their* turf. Without a solid bridge to the younger generations, are we inadvertently putting these sheep in danger of becoming food for the wild animals? The myriad sounds vying for the attention of younger women is astounding. How will they distinguish between the voice of the Good Shepherd and the voice of the thieves?

My heart aches as I meet women who have not found their Christian community to be a place of safety, but instead have found shepherds who were apathetic or harsh. Although I understand the urge to minister in arenas of comfort and familiarity, we cannot ignore the strong message of Ezekiel 34:5–6, 28–29. There we can see the impact of poor shepherding.

The sheep are

- scattered
- plundered, becoming food for wild animals
- victims of famine
- afraid
- objects of scorn
- without hope of rescue

Women in pain are wandering "over all the mountains and on every high hill" (Ezekiel 34:6). They are "scattered on a day of clouds and darkness" (v. 12) and no one is looking for them (v. 6). They are victims of famine, afraid, and often ashamed. They have been used, abused, and refused. They are thirsty for spiritual life, searching in unsafe places for a drink of water. The contaminated water they find increases their pain and extends their illness. The ones who should be leading them to the Living Water have abandoned them.

four essential elements of good shepherding

What would our ministry to women look like if our objectives were those the Lord describes in Ezekiel 34:14–16? We would

1. feed the healthy,
2. strengthen the young and the weak,
3. heal and bind up the injured, and
4. search and care for the lost.

What if we were to try a model of women's ministry structured along these four branches? What if we were to focus on shepherding the young, injured, and lost to purposefully bring them to a place of health? What if we were to find women with the spiritual gifts needed to shepherd women? What if we were to give these women greater awareness and understanding of the issues that cause women injury? What if we studied the example of the Good Shepherd to prepare these women to shepherd other women? The results would show benefits. Indeed, if every program, meeting, study, or event fit into one of these four areas—*feeding, strengthening, healing,* and *searching and caring*—we could be sure we were providing God-honoring, balanced pastoral care to our women.

Healthy Sheep Need Food

Just as healthy sheep need food to stay healthy, so healthy women need good food to stay healthy. A steady diet and nurturing climate that foster maturity and spiritual strength should form the foundation of our ministry to women. However, the menu selection should include items that keep in mind sheep that are young, injured, or lost. Women need to know what a godly woman looks like in this century. How does godliness in a feminine body cope with the stress and struggles of life today? Good shepherds provide food that is palatable, accessible, and needful. What are the needs of *your* women? When you serve food to your family or friends, certainly you ask this question before you purchase and prepare the meal. Should we do any less for the sheep God has entrusted to us?

Young Sheep Need Strengthening

There are two very strong reasons to shepherd the young. The first reason is to prevent scattering and injury. As Ezekiel has so aptly painted a picture of destruction and death to animals not protected, we realize the young are particularly vulnerable. They lack the life experience and maturity to maneuver through difficult terrain. Their search for adventure and excitement often takes them to dangerous ravines. Godly role models are scarce; many have not had healthy parentage. This applies to those who are young physically (teens, college age, young moms), and to those who are young spiritually. Who will take seriously the Lord's call to disciple, to mentor, to shepherd these precious lambs?

He tends his flock like a shepherd:
He gathers the lambs in his arms
and carries them close to his heart;
he gently leads those that have young.
(Isaiah 40:11)

Our Lord has a special heart for the young.

The second reason to shepherd the young is to prepare them to nurture the next generation. They will be the parents! How well are we passing the baton of godliness? You and I are vital team players in the handoff! Younger women in this generation are seeking older women. They *want* spiritual guidance and moral mores to follow.

What would our ministry look like if we considered young women an integral part of our programs and plans? What Bible study choices would we make? Small group options? Retreat plans? When does a young woman feel a part of women's ministry? Does she have to be married? Have children? May I suggest we intentionally draw the young into our ministries, that we proactively shepherd the young.

Lost Sheep Need to Be Found

Women need to meet Jesus! They need to know the joy of forgiveness and a relationship with the Good Shepherd! They need to experience the resurrection power in their lives. Only a relationship with the Lord can complete what a woman needs for health and wholeness! Women need a sense of connection, of friendship, and healthy relationships. They need understanding and acceptance in community.

Eddie Gibbs says we are more like Little Bo Peep than the Good Shepherd.[2] The Good Shepherd left the ninety-nine sheep to search for the one lost lamb. Little Bo Peep "has lost her sheep and can't tell where to find them." She has left them alone hoping "they will come home wagging their tails behind them." Little Bo Peep may still be waiting. Jesus came to seek and save the lost. Notice that Jesus didn't have a big spring luncheon and hope the lost sheep would show up. He went out searching for the lost one. Christmas desserts are great places to invite friends and pre-Christians, but rarely will a lost one find her way there on her own. "Home" for many lost sheep would not be our church programs. Jesus' hands and feet need to go out searching for the lost sheep! Lost sheep need to be found!

Injured Sheep Need to Be Healed

Most of the focus of this book is on injured sheep. When we think of pastoral care, we think of hurting people, and rightly so, although effective pastoral care is also given to "healthy" sheep. How much of your ministry to women is focused on "binding up the injured"?

Many women are still in places of "darkness." The Enemy has taken advantage of the pain of violation, rejection, loss, betrayal, and disillusionment. The additional misunderstanding, marginalization, and projection of guilt from spiritual leaders intensify the pain, with the result that these women become easy prey. They need a safe place to be known and yet accepted, a place to heal. They need to feel the loving arms of the Good Shepherd when the pain feels all-consuming. Injured sheep need healing!

This critical pattern of healing the injured is illustrated in the movie *The Horse Whisperer*. Grace and her horse, Pilgrim, suffered severe trauma when Pilgrim slipped off the side of a snow-covered mountain and fell into the pathway of an oncoming semi-truck. As a result of the accident, Grace lost a leg and Pilgrim's life was at risk. Pilgrim survived physically, but psychologically she was frightened and wouldn't let anyone near her for fear she would be hurt again. Neither strong demands nor physical force worked. It took someone who understood horses and trauma, cattleman Tom Booker, to bring Pilgrim back to health. Tom's patient waiting and gentle speaking and stroking communicated a message of care and understanding to Pilgrim. Eventually this opened the door for instruction toward recovery.

Grace's relationship with her mom, Annie, had deteriorated to near silence since the accident. Tom's gentle approach with Pilgrim greatly influenced Annie, a high-powered *New Yorker* magazine editor, to exchange directive demands for emotional tenderness and compassion toward her daughter. The door opened when Annie's strong exterior gave way to expressions of her own emotional pain, assuring Grace she did understand like-pain. As a result, the relationship was restored, which was essential for Grace's physical and psychological healing. In the same way, a shepherd's expressions of care for the person and her pain must precede words of instruction.

Many women are lost, injured, and young—and the healthy women need to *remain* healthy so they can shepherd them! The good news for Israel and for us is that God says, "I myself will search for my sheep and look after them. . . . I will rescue them from all the places where they were scattered on a day of clouds and darkness" (Ezekiel 34:11–12).

What joy when the Good Shepherd cares for the flock! Search out the nuggets of truth in Ezekiel 34:11–29 with me. How many benefits can you find?

The Good Shepherd

- searches for and rescues the sheep
- cares for the sheep, leading them to rest
- feeds the sheep in rich pasturelands
- searches for the lost and brings back the strays; binds up the injured and strengthens the weak
- gives peace
- rids the land of wild beasts
- protects the sheep so that they can live and sleep in safety
- blesses the sheep and provides fruit
- sends showers of blessings
- provides security
- breaks the yoke, rescues the sheep from enslavement, protects the sheep from being plundered and devoured by wild animals

- causes the sheep to live in safety; allows no one to make them afraid
- frees the sheep from being the victims of famine and the objects of scorn
- provides for their needs

The sovereign Lord concludes:

Then they will know that I, the LORD their God, am with them and that they, the house of Israel, are my people. . . . You my sheep, the sheep of my pasture, are people, and I am your God. (Ezekiel 34:30–31)

Can you imagine the women of your church and community experiencing even a few of the blessings on this list? Imagine women finding places of safety, places to embrace Christ and gain health. Imagine these healthy women, who understand pain and the joy of healing, becoming shepherds to young, injured, and lost women. Certainly women would impact their culture in the way Paul exhorts Titus to impact the decadent society of Crete!

❦   ❦   ❦

Although Sandy wanted to believe such a good shepherd existed, the damage of poor shepherding created immobilizing doubts. A co-worker consistently expressed love to her and occasionally invited her to church. Sandy eventually went with her and accepted Christ as her Savior! What joy flooded her soul as she found the Living Water she had been thirsting for for more than twenty years! Although it took time to change many of the messages she received in her previous religious experience, she had a hunger for biblical truth.

Unlike Sandy, her husband wanted no part of another "religious" experience. He had given up a professional baseball career (at the insistence "of the previous institution") to be a leader in their "religious program." He was angry with God and "organized religion."

Sandy's desire for her husband's salvation grew, as did her daily prayer for him. She found several women in her new church who shared her concern. They agreed to meet weekly to pray. Sandy was surprised to find God responding to her prayers by doing a deep work in her life. Sandy valued the women who came alongside her and walked with her through the maze of biblical misunderstandings and personal deceptions she had encountered. These shepherds provided a safe place, understanding, and personal integrity. They encouraged Sandy to find the answers in the Bible and to share her findings.

Sandy, along with a group of women in her church, began to see the power of prayer. Their own daily dependence upon God to be godly in their homes drew their husbands to the well of Living Water. Sandy's husband was the first to accept Christ.

Nearly twelve years later, God has used Sandy to begin a *Women at Rest Ministry* for women who want to influence their home for Christ. Sandy believes the gentle shepherding of the women in that first group was the key to bringing health to a critically injured sheep. They broke the yoke of enslavement and rescued Sandy from being "plundered and devoured by the wild animals." Sandy's life is a beautiful example of a lost, injured sheep that was brought into the fold by authentic shepherding.

THE GOOD SHEPHERD IN JOHN 10

The key components of the women who shepherded Sandy reflect characteristics of the Good Shepherd found in John 10. You may want to explore this text and then make a list of characteristics. As we spend time with Jesus, we will acquire those characteristics. How are you doing? Are you beginning to look like the Good Shepherd?

1. The Good Shepherd has integrity.

The shepherd of the flock is a person of integrity. That is the reason he enters by the gate (John 10:1–4). Whenever the shepherd comes to the fold, it is for the benefit of the sheep—he always comes with beneficial intentions. The sheep do not fear him.[3] Whether a shepherd whistles, gently calls, sings a tune, or taps on the gate, he does so intentionally to alert the sheep of his arrival. The owner's entry seeks to enrich his sheep, and they welcome his arrival.

This is unlike the predator, who wants to catch the sheep off guard. The one who finds other ways to enter is a thief, a robber. His intent is selfish and his approach deceptive. His purpose—to steal, kill, and destroy—is counter to the purpose of the Good Shepherd, which is to give life. The true shepherd's role is known to the sheep. He is a person of integrity.

Integrity was central to Sandy's health. Although it took time to reprogram her mental messages, her fears were slowly put to rest as women of integrity ministered to her need.

2. The Good Shepherd is relationally authentic and accessible.

The Good Shepherd calls His sheep by name. He knows them and they know Him (John 10:3–5). Authentic relationship is key for the sheep and their shepherd.

The sheep recognize their shepherd's voice. The sheep have become "conditioned to the familiar nuances and personal accent of their shepherd's call. . . . They actually run toward the shepherd. They come to him for they know he has something good for them."[4] He may call them to fresh pastures or shelter from a storm. He may supply them with fresh feed, salt, or water. He may examine them to make sure they are fit and flourishing. The sheep's welfare is of utmost importance to the shepherd, and the sheep can expect the shepherd to be available for their benefit.

The Good Shepherd knows and is known. The sheep are dependent upon the shepherd for a diet and climate that promote growth. The shepherd is dependent upon the sheep for wool. Since neither can produce a genuine version of the needed articles alone, they have an interdependent relationship. Their relationship is mutually beneficial.

The journey of life developmentally and spiritually progresses from dependence, through independence, to interdependence.

Relational authenticity and accessibility promote interdependence. Interdependence is further enhanced through clear boundary definition. Recognition of the mutual benefits motivates sheep and shepherd to continually explore ways of authentically relating to one another.

This is especially true for shepherds of women. Women flourish in interdependent relationships, especially authentic, accessible relationships!

3. The Good Shepherd is a leader.

The Good Shepherd leads the sheep out; He goes ahead of them (John 10:3–4). The shepherd knows where the sheep need to go. He anticipates their needs. He has explored fresh pasture or shelter from the storm. He leads them to places of shelter, recovery, and health. (You may want to explore further elements of provision in Isaiah 30:15–26.)

By definition, good shepherds of women will assume a gentle leadership role. Women of integrity who have experienced emotional pain, been healed, gained understanding, and received training will be excellent shepherds because they have already traveled down the path of pain to wholeness. They are role models to women in pain. Women who are healthy, reproducing disciples will lead the way for younger women. Those who know Christ can introduce Him to others. In the same way that a shepherd is continually looking for fresh pasture and healthy environments for his sheep, a shepherd of women will be teachable, looking for more effective ways to minister.

4. The Good Shepherd is committed.

The Good Shepherd has come "that they may have life, and have it to the full. . . . I lay down my life for the sheep" (John 10:10, 15). Jesus gave His life so that we might have life. Is not that reason enough to give my life to serve His purpose?

Shepherding will cost. Fruit yield is often delayed. Commitment to the Good Shepherd is essential for the task. It is more than "a good idea"! Knowing it is the life of Jesus in us that we are pouring into others makes it an *imperative!*

four examples of good shepherding

Elizabeth

Elizabeth, a relative of Mary the mother of Jesus, exhibited these four shepherding qualities in the early days of Mary's pregnancy. Luke describes Elizabeth and her husband as "upright in the sight of God, observing all the Lord's commandments and regulations blamelessly" (Luke 1:6). This woman was able to maintain her integrity through the many years of infertility. Elizabeth lived in a culture that believed barrenness was in direct response to God's displeasure and/or the woman's sin. Day after day and year after year Elizabeth must have felt the pain of empty arms and judgmental neighbors. Yet she maintained her integrity before God.

In her old age Elizabeth became pregnant, and in her sixth month Gabriel arrived with news of Mary's pregnancy. Gabriel's message to Mary concluded with these words: "Even Elizabeth your relative is going to have a child in her old age, and she who was said to be barren is in her sixth month. For nothing is impossible with God" (Luke 1:36–37). Gabriel cited Elizabeth as a living example of God's impossible work!

In God's perfect timing, He provided an older woman who was relationally authentic and accessible and able to shepherd Mary through the uncertainties of societal shame. Elizabeth knew shame because she was *not* pregnant, and now Mary would feel shame because she *was*. Elizabeth may have talked about hurtful experiences of misunderstanding and community prejudice. She may have strengthened Mary for the days ahead. Can you imagine the emotional conversations, the tears, and the prayers these two women shared during those precious three months together? Can you see them comparing family photo albums, wondering who in their families the precious sons growing in their bodies would look like? Can you see them laughing and singing songs of joy together—to the point of falling on the couch exhausted—emptying glass after glass of iced tea?

Take some time and make a list of the similarities and differences in these two women. You will be encouraged to see how growth flourishes when life circumstances between women are dissimilar yet the call is similar. Both Mary and Elizabeth were women of integrity, committed to the Lord. Elizabeth's experience qualified her as God's choice shepherd to Mary at a critical time in this young woman's life, at a critical time in the history of the world.

Sandy

In a similar way, today Sandy shepherds women because she was shepherded by women of integrity who were relationally authentic, accessible, willing to gently lead, and committed to the Good Shepherd.

A Shepherd of Women

The profile of a shepherd of women is strikingly like that of the Good Shepherd. The shepherd of women knows that "the Lord is my Shepherd." As she spends time in His presence, drawing on the provisions of Psalm 23, she more easily leads women to the Chief Shepherd of our souls. She knows the ultimate consummation of this relationship, as beautifully described in Revelation 7:16–17:

> *Never again will they hunger;*
> *never again will they thirst.*

The sun will not beat upon them,
> *nor any scorching heat.*
For the Lamb at the center of the throne will be their shepherd;
> *he will lead them to springs of living water.*
And God will wipe away every tear from their eyes.

She understands the provisions of Psalm 23:

> The Lord is my shepherd . . .
>> He makes me lie down
>> He leads me
>> He restores my soul (soul provision)
>> He guides me (spiritual provision)
>> He is with me
>> He comforts me
>> He prepares a banquet for me (physical provision)
>> He anoints me as the honored guest

> As a result . . .
>> I will not be in want
>> I will fear no evil
>> I will dwell in the house of the Lord forever

Mary of Magdala

Certainly this psalm reflects the personal experience of Mary of Magdala. She may have spent more time with Jesus than any other woman in the Gospels.[5] Although we do not know the full impact on her life of Jesus' casting seven demons out of her, the contrast must have been great. Her devotion to the Lord was exemplary. When everyone else walked out, Mary Magdalene stayed.

Mary Magdalene was part of the group of women that traveled with Jesus and the disciples. "These women were helping to support them out of their own means" (Luke 8:3). Whether Mary Magdalene was a financially independent woman, or whether she contributed in other ways to the needs of the group, we find Mary Magdalene's name at the beginning of nearly every list of women traveling with Jesus. Given Mary Magdalene's dependable presence and her influence in leading the women during the last days of Jesus' presence on earth, she undoubtedly had a shepherding role with this group of women.

The powerful impact of Mary Magdalene can be understood

by emulating her pattern as a shepherd. When Jesus was crucified and buried and His closest followers had fled, we find Mary Magdalene *lingering* at the cross, *lingering* at His burial, and *lingering* at the empty tomb. After Jesus rose from the dead, Mary Magdalene was the first person to see Him, to hear Him call her by name, to receive His commission, to proclaim His resurrection to His followers.

In the same way, *lingering in the presence of the Good Shepherd* is the best way to reflect the profile of a good shepherd.

Once the foundation of *lingering* is laid and maintained, a good shepherd will develop other skills that enable her to shepherd well. Our next chapter further identifies some of those skills.

the skill of shepherding women

marianne, the adopted adult daughter of a long-standing church family member, seemed to be the perfect example of self-fulfilling prophecy. Once she made a poor choice, family members shook their heads and predicted she would be like her biological father. One choice led to two, then three, and eventually the die seemed cast.

When I met Marianne, I was a young, inexperienced pastor's wife determined that Marianne could turn the ship of her life around, given enough positive input and encouragement. I set out to fill the role of Marianne's personal encourager.

Marianne freely described the sordid details of her single life. Without hesitation she told me about the three different men (none of whom married her) who had fathered her three children. The most recent man in her life was currently in prison. Even Marianne's competence as a social worker did not bring order out of chaos in her life. No one could make her life work.

I began by telling her I cared and that I wanted to spend time with her. She called me regularly and talked until I ended the conversation, often one or two hours later. I wanted to "be there for her." Each time I had a suggestion, or gave input, she assured me that she had tried that. Initially, I assumed that her family and friends were too quickly judging her, not giving her the positive input she needed to move forward. But after several months, I realized that Marianne had no intention of changing her life. She *liked* her life the way it was. She enjoyed being center stage in family head-shaking and "What are we going to do with Marianne?" discussions. Her adventures provided new family stories. It was her role in the family system. It was what she knew best.

GUIDELINES FOR SHEPHERDS

Through that draining experience I developed guidelines for shepherding—nine dos and nine don'ts.

SOME IMPORTANT DOS

1. Do discover if she really wants to grow or change.

We cannot assume that because people like talking about their problems, they actually want to move forward. Giving Marianne suggestions, asking questions of her, and giving her options were ways to discover her level of interest in changing her lifestyle. She not only did not want to receive input, she did not follow through with suggested options. Simply giving more encouragement and positive input are not magical formulas. The Mariannes in our communities can potentially drain even the best-intentioned shepherd. Shepherds need to set and hold clear boundaries, while evaluating their ministry priorities.

Look for women with teachable spirits, women who want to move forward and will follow through with the suggestions or homework you have given them. Offer to meet a second or third time only *after* they have completed a reading or made a suggested contact.

2. Do know "What I can do" and "What I cannot do."[1]

Make your own list for each situation. The following list is only an example.

What I can do	What I cannot do
1. Be a listener	1. Change her
2. Designate time to be available	2. Go without regular sleep
3. Get more help	3. Do it all alone
4. Pray for her	4. Cure her hurts or fix it
5. Suggest professional help	5. Erase past pain/choices

Share this list verbally with the women you are shepherding. This list would have helped Marianne and me by forcing us to set healthy boundaries and realistic expectations. Unlimited listening time and twenty-four/seven availability alone are not the solution to another's problems. Checking the list when I felt the urge to fix her problems would have confirmed my decision to do only "What I can do" while acknowledging "What I cannot do."

3. Do know that another's pain may make you feel uncomfortable.

Remind yourself that even though another's pain might not be something you enjoy seeing, it might be a necessary part of that person's growing.

A woman will go to the dentist's office to get relief from a toothache. Once the Novocain is injected and the mouth numbed, the pain is gone. Should the woman believe she no longer needs the dentist's work because the pain is relieved, she will likely experience pain again within a few hours. A delay in dealing with the root problem may actually intensify the decay, which will extend the pain while further limiting repair options. Simply relieving a woman's pain may not be the most helpful care.

Although it was tough to watch Cindy go through a painful divorce, it was obvious she wanted God to use it for spiritual growth in her life—and He did! Often it is in a painful place that God gets our best attention. To relieve the pain may be to rob a woman of God's best work in her life. Instead, walking alongside her *in* the pain is the work of a good shepherd. Note that your own discomfort with her pain is not always an indication that you need to relieve her of it. (Emotional, physical, and sexual abuse are certainly exceptions to this point. If a woman is in immediate danger of abuse, she certainly needs to be relieved of the danger of that kind of pain.)

4. Do know your own limits.

Know your best shepherding skills. Know your weaknesses or areas of limitation. If possible, enlist the support of others to cover areas where you are weak. Linda realized she had little understanding of the pain of divorce but was naturally drawn to women experiencing the death of a spouse. She had been widowed twice and knew her strengths were primarily in that area. She also knew her listening skills were more acute in the daytime, rather than in the evening.

Sally knew her strengths were in providing practical help to women in pain: meals, cleaning, and transportation. Jane preferred giving her presence to a woman in pain. She wanted to sit beside her, listen, wait, or pray. Jane is at her best later in the day. Jane often asked Sally to provide practical help, and Sally appreciated Jane's bedside manner in a crisis. These shepherds were able to maximize their energies by moving into situations within their own strengths while soliciting help for their areas of limitation.

5. Do know referral resources.

Have a readily available list of professional counselors by area of specialty. Often women in pain are best served by giving them credible resources and the assurance of your continued support and care. Compile a list of reputable resources by calling or interviewing local counselors. Ask for referrals from friends or pastors in your area.

Be sure to have "hot line" and shelter numbers for emergency physical and sexual abuse situations.

Although Marinda had experienced sexual abuse and could shepherd Patty through her journey of incest recovery, she knew the real work of Patty's recovery required professional help. Patty was grateful that Marinda knew the value of having someone walking alongside her as a shepherd while she herself did the deeper work with a professional counselor.

One of the dangers of being a shepherd of women is assuming that the ability or responsibility to restore women to health belongs to the shepherd alone. The Good Samaritan enlisted the help of the innkeeper. The paralytic of Mark 2 had the help of four friends who brought him to Jesus for healing. None of these good helpers brought healing alone, but with the help of community they were able to find the needed resources that resulted in healing. A shepherd of women must know and use referral resources.

6. Do know you will not have all the answers.

Often women fear they need all the answers before they can reach out with help. In actuality, women most often need a listening ear and an empathetic response. Prayer and coaching may follow, but having all the answers will not. You cannot be her savior, nor should you try to be. Someone has said, "There is a God and you ain't Him!" The Savior role is already filled. Only He has all the answers and the power to implement those solutions. The shepherd's role is to introduce the woman in pain to the Chief Shepherd!

As a shepherd you may have one piece or be the one to lead her to the next piece of the puzzle of her life. That one piece is very important, but it is *one piece.* You may have the phone number of a good counselor who will bring needed assessment of the situation. You may invite a friend who has had a similar experience to share the insights she has gained. A book or cassette tape of relevant information could be a meaningful resource. Your prayer support may be the most strategic gift you give.

Pearl felt the weight of the world had been lifted from her

shoulders after meeting with Simbala. Simbala was the first woman who listened—who really listened—and seemed to understand her feelings. Just knowing someone understood lightened the weight of her burden for her prodigal son. Praying together brought peace, although neither woman left knowing how God would answer.

7. Do know she has a choice.

No matter how good your perspective, wisdom, or intuition or the Bible verse you offer, remember that it is *her choice* to accept or reject it. Shepherds must respect the choice of others.

Mei-Lee had blown it with her daughter Kia. She had responded to her daughter in anger, and she knew that this anger had hurt her. Nicole's biblical suggestion that Mei-Lee apologize to her daughter and ask for forgiveness was not well received. Mei-Lee said that in her culture parents are always right and that her daughter would no longer respect her if she admitted wrong. Nicole was left to pray that the Spirit of God would change Mei-Lee's heart and that Mei-Lee would choose God's way over cultural mores. Nicole continues to express God's love to Mei-Lee while appropriately sharing her own experience of God's forgiving power.

8. Do know your presence counts.

Judith felt so alone. Her husband was in the intensive care unit after a tragic auto accident. Judith waited and waited for news of hope of recovery. The shock was still fresh. A friend of her husband's came in. He asked questions, expressed anxiety, and then talked incessantly of his relationship with Burney. Finally, when Judith was alone again, she realized that silence was preferable to relentless talking.

Then Lois came and just sat beside Judith. With an occasional hand on her shoulder, a smile, and a warm glance, Lois' presence communicated peace, love, and the calm assurance that Judith was not alone. Lois' prayer lifted Judith's thoughts to God and led her to feel His presence through Lois' shepherding. Of all the people who came to the hospital during the remaining days, Judith remembers none ministering so powerfully as her new friend Lois. Know that your presence does count!

The presence of Job's friends Eliphaz, Bildad, and Zophar was exemplary during the first seven days of their encounter. "They set out from their homes and met together by agreement to go and sympathize with him and comfort him." When they saw Job, "they could hardly recognize him." The change was so stark, "they began to weep aloud, and . . . tore their robes and sprinkled dust on their heads. Then they sat on the ground with him for seven days and nights" in silence "because they saw how great his suffering was" (Job 2:11–13). They identified with Job's grief and calamity. Their presence was a comfort during that first week of silent sympathy.

9. Do know your God is powerful!

He is the Redeemer. He is the Great Physician, the Healer. He is the One who brings Life. He *does* answer prayer! A shepherd of women simply leads women to the Chief Shepherd. There is only one Savior, Jesus Christ the Lord. Shepherds of women may be tempted to move into the role of savior or messiah. Women want to help; it is in their very nature to want to help others. But an effective shepherd of women remembers that she is to take a woman's hand and place it in God's hand.

Lily's marriage was at risk. Bonnie understood some of the conflicts and recommended a marriage seminar. Lily and her husband went, followed by marriage counseling. The lack of visible progress diminished hope. Bonnie's pastor agreed to meet with the couple. Through the power of prayer and the work of the Holy Spirit, the pastor brought to the surface the hidden source of anger in Lily's life. This anger had infected her perspective and spilled into the family dynamic. That revelation was the missing piece that brought healing and reconciliation to a near-divorce relationship. All agreed it was God's work in answer to prayer that revealed the key to recovery. Our God is powerful!

SOME IMPORTANT DON'TS

1. Don't be quick to give advice.

Most women are not looking for advice, and those who are would do better to discover the next step themselves through your wise questioning. People are more likely to make the hard decision to change when they have discovered the needed change themselves. Coaching women through the process is our most effective strategy. Asking questions such as "What are you going to do? What are your options?" walk women through the process of good decision making. (See the section "Reflect—There Is Hope" in this chapter for more reflective questions.) Offering advice keeps a woman dependent on you for further decision making.

2. Don't make promises you cannot keep.

"I'll be here night and day for you" is a gallant promise, but is it one you can realistically keep? Can you be sure that "it will be all right?" If not, it would be better not to declare it so. It is more devastating to promise that you will always be there and then not be there than to not offer that kind of open-ended commitment. A primary need for a woman in emotional pain is stability and trustworthiness. Be sure you will be available when you say you will.

3. Don't try to fix her or her problem.

This is simply not possible and sets both of you up for disappointment and possible disillusionment. It is also exhausting!

Elizabeth's mother continues to hold Elizabeth hostage emotionally. Tears follow nearly every phone call. Although they live miles apart, the pain of Elizabeth's mother's words immobilize her adult daughter.

Elizabeth's neighbor, Celeste, expresses her anger at the way Elizabeth's mother causes Elizabeth pain. After every phone call, Celeste is quick to tell Elizabeth what she should say or do.

Seeing a friend continue in pain is difficult. Our immediate impulse is to fix the situation. However, no matter how hard she tries, Celeste cannot fix Elizabeth.

Elizabeth needs to embrace the fact that she has choices. She needs to understand that she is a person worthy of respect, and that once she begins treating herself respectfully, she will empower others to do the same. Setting boundaries is one way of showing respect. Once Elizabeth grasps the truth of how God respects and loves her, she may be able to respect herself enough to communicate that respect to her mother.

This is not something Celeste can do for her, much as she wants to. Celeste can expose Elizabeth to the truth and pray for her, but Celeste is powerless to fix Elizabeth or her problem.

4. Don't make assumptions.

Ask questions to discover feelings and facts. Keep a learning posture so that you can clearly hear the perspective of the woman in pain. Always ask a woman who seems depressed if she has had a recent medical checkup. Don't assume she is in good physical health. The cause of her depression could be physical or hormonal.

5. Don't assume the story you hear is the story.

There are usually three stories: her story, another's story, and reality. The important story is the woman's *perspective.* The truth is probably somewhere in the middle of what she and her friend, mother, or father say. We each deal with life as we see it. Her perspective is the reality she deals with every day. It is knowing her reality that will enable a shepherd to walk her through her painful circumstances. Understanding that there may be another perspective will also be essential in leading her to a place of healing and strength.

6. Don't make premature judgments.

Hold your judgment on the person causing her pain until you have opportunity to interface with that person. The patience to do this often comes after a shepherd has had a few experiences of incorrect judgments made on the basis of one woman's perspective. Don't place blame quickly. Ask the Holy Spirit for discernment and rest in His wisdom.

Hold your judgment also on a woman in pain, realizing that people react differently in a crisis than they do in a comfort zone. Understand that a different woman may emerge in an accepting environment.

7. Don't do all the work.

It is important to remember it is her problem, her pain, and she must own it. She is the only one who can make the hard choices that will bring healing or change. A shepherd brings encouragement and prayer, but the woman in pain must do her part.

Elisa suspected something when her forty-year-old husband's sexual requests increased threefold in a given day. Finally in desperation Elisa asked a woman's retreat speaker from out of town the best way to respond to these impossible sexual demands. The fact that her husband was likely caught in the web of pornography was difficult for Elisa to accept. She needed someone who understood and could help her see this heartbreaking reality. Elisa was fearful of the future. The grief of betrayal and infidelity threatened to overwhelm her. In this stage of shock and anger, Elisa needed a shepherd who could invest time in care and prayer at this stage of her pain.

It was important for Elisa to understand that her husband had a sexual addiction problem. His sexual addiction was neither caused by anything Elisa had done nor would it end as a result of Elisa's being more sexually responsive, more submissive, or a better homemaker. It was his addiction, and only he could work to change that.

Once Elisa gained more understanding and courage, she knew she needed to confront her husband. She could enable him to continue his addictive pattern by covering for him or she could hold him accountable for his choices. At this point in the process, her work would increase and her support base would also need to increase. With the help of her shepherd, she was able to locate a counselor and support group for her husband, should he choose to get help. Elisa began setting boundaries and accountability structures. It was critical that Elisa do this work and not remain dependent on the initial work of her shepherd.

The amount of healing work a woman in pain can do will

crescendo as the initial shock of grief subsides. The shepherd may carry the biggest load in the beginning. The danger is in this pattern continuing long-term by encouraging the woman in pain to become dependent, rather than interdependent.

8. Don't spiritualize everything.

This will call for the discernment of the Holy Spirit. There is a time when it is appropriate to give Scripture and biblical wisdom—don't miss it! There is also a time when a woman in emotional pain is not ready to hear the reasons for Job's misery. She is not ready to hear spiritual reasons or the benefits of the pain she is in.

During the first few weeks of crisis Katharine was not ready to hear how (or "that") God might use her experience of a son in prison to minister to others. In fact, she clearly declared, "Don't even begin to tell me how God will use this! I don't want to help other mothers with this! That is not a good enough reason for my son to go to prison!" Once she is further along in the journey, the time may be right. Be sensitive to the Spirit's leading! Keep praying!

Don't be afraid to admit you don't have all the answers. Confess that you too would like to know the "why." In the middle of the questions, a shepherd can confidently assure a woman in pain that she is not alone. God is aware of her circumstance. God is present and He cares.

9. Don't carry all the emotional weight.

A role-play for shepherd training reveals a final important guideline for shepherds of women.

In this role-play, Kerri enters with a full backpack. She removes the backpack, opens it, and begins taking out each item. As she removes an item, she expresses the aspect of emotional pain it represents.

Kerri's family was going through crisis. Her absent father accentuated her mother's strong control. Kerri was feeling responsible and crumbling under the load. Kerri unpacked tissues representing tears, insect repellent representing her repulsion to certain family members, a first aid kit representing her need for help, eyeglasses to visualize her need for clearer perspective, a small candle to bring insight into her situation, a knife depicting the sharp pain she feels when her parents fight, and a phone to represent her need to talk to someone.

As Kerri unpacks each item she puts it into Mrs. Wong's hand as she talks about the pain it represents. Mrs. Wong, Kerri's pastor's wife, is now left with each of Kerri's problems. Will Mrs. Wong take each item and place them into her own backpack, taking them home with her?

Mrs. Wong remembers that verse 2 of Galatians 6 says, "Carry each other's burdens," and yet verse 5 says, "Each one should carry his own load." These seem contradictory. What should she do?

This seeming contradiction may be clarified by an illustration from my husband, Jim. During his years of being a summer canoe instructor, Jim told campers preparing for a canoe trip to each carry their own backpack filled with a sandwich, sunscreen, and a towel. In the same way, we each have a responsibility to carry our daily load.

But a canoe is too heavy for one camper. Three campers (with their own backpacks in place) will place themselves under a canoe, lift it off the rack, and carry it down to the water's edge. In the same way, the excess weight, the crushing loads of life are too much for one person to bear alone without help. These we carry together, in addition to our own backpacks.

Mrs. Wong, in our role-play, will listen and empathize as Kerri talks about each item. But one by one she will place the items back in Kerri's backpack. The only exception will be the phone. She agrees to stay in touch, to listen and shepherd Kerri through this rough time. She agrees to pray and together bring perspective and hope. However, the problem is still Kerri's. Mrs. Wong will relieve some of the weight of Kerri's backpack by listening and offering help. Kerri will need fewer tissues and eventually may give up the insect repellent as she works through the issues. Her load will lighten, but not by simply dumping all her problems into someone else's backpack.

skills for shepherds

A toothache or headache demands our full attention as we concentrate on easing the pain. We just want to take pain medication, crawl into bed, and be left alone. Similarly, emotional pain can make it difficult to focus on anything else. Women often want to isolate and may not pursue help. They may believe no one could possibly understand or that an offer of help implies that they are not handling life very well.

Isolation may actually compound the emotional pain with feelings of being the only one who has felt this pain. Women often take "pain relievers." These may be spending sprees, overeating, alcohol, or drugs—anything that will numb the pain. This further exacerbates the pain of isolation and the desire to hide not only the painful issue but the "pain relievers" as well.

Women need to know they are not alone and someone does understand. Listening to a woman's pain is one of the most effective ways of breaking through feelings of isolation and misunderstanding.

ACTIVE LISTENING—I AM NOT ALONE

Active listening requires a different set of skills than is generally employed in grocery store conversations. Listening in the produce aisle generally means rehearsing what I will say as soon as there is a pause in the conversation. We may "cross talk." As she gives more of her story, I am giving her more of mine. Two separate conversations may be occurring, and an observer might wonder how much is actually being heard by the other speaker.

A second listening pattern may be that of looking for the flaw in the other person's thinking with the intent of "straightening her out." We take the position of conversation police, giving tickets for infringements of feeling and thought.

A third and certainly more effective listening style is "active listening." The listening is not focused on how the listener will respond or even on policing the speaker's thought process. Rather, the focus is to *truly understand* what the speaker is feeling and thinking. An active listener listens for facts, but more importantly for feelings and thoughts behind the facts. The listener gives attention to all communication, verbal and nonverbal. Then she *reflects* what the speaker has communicated.

1. The active listener will listen with her ears.

She will listen for facts. She will hear the presenting problem, realizing it may not be the real problem. A shepherd will listen for words that express feeling and perception. A woman's perception is reality to her, and that reality will evoke feelings and responses for action. A shepherd listens for intonation and voice inflection. She also listens for an absence of feeling or perception.

Jerrylyn's presenting situation was an out-of-state move due to a "dream" job promotion. Mary Ann understood transitions and was prepared to shepherd Jerrylyn through this move. However, as Mary Ann "heard" an absence of excitement over what should have been a celebrative response to a dream job, Mary Ann began to suspect an underlying problem. As Mary Ann gently explored, she uncovered Jerrylyn's excruciating pain surrounding leaving "friends" behind.

Mary Ann essentially opened the door for Jerrylyn to reveal a yearlong secret that was putting a trusted neighbor's marriage at risk. Jerrylyn's well-kept secret was eating her alive. She needed someone to process the pain and support her decision to repent. Mary Ann's active listening told Jerrylyn she was not alone. Mary Ann's ability to hear an "absence of feeling" is critical in good shepherding.

The active listener will gently respond with one- or two-word phrases that will encourage the speaker to talk. Phrases such as: "uh huh," "yes," "go on," "I see," "and then?" This will assure the speaker that the listener is engaged and cares, which is vital for a woman in pain. Often a woman in emotional pain feels confused about her own feelings. She may believe she is confusing her listener as well. If this is confirmed by her listener's silence or inappropriate responses, it will likely close her down.

2. The active listener will listen with her eyes.

She will look for nonverbal clues. Approximately 85–90 percent of communication is nonverbal. The position of a woman's body—sitting on the edge of her chair, sitting back in a relaxed position, slumped over or head held high—communicates feelings. A woman's facial expressions may betray or confirm her verbal communication. Looking away from the listener, giving the floor or wall eye contact may suggest discomfort or shame. If this woman's "normal" demeanor is known, deviations from that normal are telling.

Terry's lighthearted descriptions and laughter alone would have led Susan to believe Terry was coping quite well with the recent death of her mother. But Terry's uncharacteristic disheveled appearance, along with her red eyes and tired look, alerted Susan to hidden pain. Terry's need to know she was not alone in this hard place opened the door for her to process the pain.

The active listener will give good eye contact. She will lean forward toward the speaker and look into her eyes. She will resist distractions in the room or out the window. A repeated eye movement away from the speaker may suggest to the speaker that the listener has a lack of interest or discomfort with the speaker's pain. The active listener will maintain an open posture, resist folding arms. She will communicate warmth through gentle facial expressions of understanding that reflect the feelings of the speaker.

3. The active listener will listen with her heart.

She will enter into the speaker's world with the intent of knowing what it feels like to be in her experience. The listener's awareness of her own feelings of loss, anger, and fear, for example, are critically important in understanding the feelings of others. Empathy is the result of listening with the heart.

Maria thought she "should be able to handle this." She believed a mature Christian should be able to "be strong" in the midst of trials. If she were just a better Christian her husband would love her more. Sonia's own journey with physical abuse enabled her to understand the cycle of "love-hate" feelings Maria had toward her husband. Sonia remembered feeling it was all her fault. She was able to "listen with her heart." Sonia gave Maria permission to acknowledge the paradoxical feelings, to open Maria's eyes to the reality of the abuse cycle, and to understand it was not her fault. Maria eventually began to see it was her husband who had a control/anger problem and she had been enabling him. It was Sonia's empathetic responses that led Maria to see the truth of her painful situation and to assure Maria she was not alone.

A shepherd who uses active listening skills communicates an essential message to women in pain: *You are not alone.* Questions and responses that help will include the following (see appendix C for more active listening exercises):

1. "Are you feeling _____?" Use a word that is weaker in intensity than you sense she feels. This gives her the opportunity to express the intensity of her feelings. By using a stronger word you may risk leading her to believe she should have stronger feelings in this situation, or that you interpret her feelings as "worse" than they really are. Find a list of feeling words if you have difficulty generating them on your own (see appendix E, "A List of Feeling Words").

2. "You sound _____."

3. "Are you saying that _____."

4. "Sounds like _____."

These questions provide opportunity for the listener to repeat, paraphrase, or summarize. It is important to be sure the listener clearly hears and understands the meaning behind what the woman in pain is saying before the listener responds. It is worth taking time to repeat or paraphrase before moving forward into a coaching stance.

EMPATHIZE—MY FEELINGS MATTER

A second message that is needed is *my feelings matter.* Shepherds who take their listening skills to the next step will express empathy. Webster defines *empathy* as "the intellectual identification with or vicarious experiencing of the feelings, thoughts or attitudes of another."[2]

Sonia, by entering into the feelings of Maria and having some sense of what it felt like to be in her situation, enabled Maria to feel she was understood. Sonia further confirmed the legitimacy of Maria's feelings by empathizing without judging. Sonia may have said, "Yes, I have had similar feelings," or "I am sure I would feel the same way if I'd been through what you have."

An essential prerequisite for effective empathetic response is the ability of the listener to be in touch with her own feelings.[3] If Sonia were still denying or discounting her own feelings of anxiety, anger, or loss, it would be difficult for her to accept or understand them in Maria. Rather Sonia would find them threatening and would instinctively resist or deny them. Maria's friend Rosario may not have experienced physical abuse, as Sonia did, but if Rosario has allowed herself to embrace feelings of anxiety, anger, and loss, she will be able to empathetically listen to Maria's story. Once Rosario has received understanding of the physically abusive cycle, she may offer further understanding of Maria's situation.

It is not the experience that needs experiencing, but that we have the ability to enter the feelings inherent in the experience.[4] This will require us to be authentic in our own painful experiences.

As Sonia is authentic in her acknowledgment of the pain of physical and emotional abuse in her own life, she is freer to identify it and empathize with it in the lives of other women. Conversely, if Sonia had denied the reality of physical abuse in her own life, she would probably have concurred with Maria's initial belief that she simply needed to "endure trials" and try harder at being a stronger Christian and better wife. Unfortunately, women with strong religious backgrounds often are the least likely to believe that violence against them is wrong . . . there is . . . a tendency for battered Christian women to believe they are ontologically evil and somehow deserving of the abuse they receive.[5] This approach has resulted in fatal physical harm for women with abusive husbands.

Empathetic listening enables a shepherd to
1. Enter another's world
2. Enter into another's feelings

Empathy gives a woman
1. Understanding
2. Acceptance *in* her pain

Empathetic responses
1. "That really hurts"
2. "I am so sorry" or "I am so sorry that happened to you"
3. "I love you" or "I care about you"

The Scriptures highlight the importance of listening over speaking: "Everyone should be quick to listen, slow to speak" (James 1:19). In case the point is missed, a more direct proverb says, "It's stupid and embarrassing to give an answer before you listen" (Proverbs 18:13 CEV).

REFLECT—THERE IS HOPE

Active listening calls for a shepherd to become a sounding board for a woman to think through an issue and discern what she should do. In the same way that a mirror reflects the image before it, a shepherd will reflect back to the woman in pain what she is thinking and feeling.

A shepherd may think of herself as a coach using reflection skills. She will avoid insensitive answers or direct advice. Rather she will ask questions to lead the woman in pain through a process of decision making. In this way she will impart skills that will lessen the likelihood of unhealthy dependency on the shepherd but instead strengthen the woman's own ability to cope with future emotional pain.

When Dorina's husband of forty-five years died, she felt her own life was over. Don was her confidant, encourager, partner, lover, and financier. In the ensuing months Dorina found her bank account overdrawn and her credit card limit reached. Dorina was feeling there was no hope at the time Valerie entered Dorina's life. Valerie used active listening skills to establish a relationship of trust. What Dorina needed most was hope that she would be able to survive her husband's death and restore financial health to her accounts. Valerie began by using questions similar to these.

1. What are you going to do?
2. What are your options?
3. What is the implication of that choice?
4. How will that choice impact you? Impact others?
5. What roadblocks do you anticipate? How will you move through them?
6. What resources will you need? Where will your support come from?
7. What do you want your life to be like in five years?
8. How will the choices you are making now bring you the hoped for benefits?
9. What do you think God wants you to do?
10. Where do you feel God is in all this?

Notice that all of the above questions are open-ended. None requires a yes or no answer. Open-ended questions are the preferred choice for active listening. Notice also that these questions place the presenting problem on the shoulders of the woman in pain, not the shepherd. It was not Valerie's task to figure out what Dorina should do. Valerie's role was to coach Dorina to a viable response or decision. Valerie's own experience in managing her finances responsibly gave her further insights into formulating good questions. Valerie gave Dorina hope by simply reflecting her thinking process through these strategic questions.

RESPECT—I CAN MOVE FORWARD

Respect acknowledges that every human being is an image bearer. Each person should be treated with respect and dignity. Respect informs me she has the ability to feel and make choices differently than me. She alone has the ability to change herself. She alone is responsible for her "stuff." There are limits to what I can do for her. I cannot embrace salvation through Jesus Christ for her. I cannot choose faith or morality for her.

Valerie's acceptance of who Dorina is gives her the freedom to change. Valerie's belief in Dorina's ability to make changes through good choices gives Dorina hope and the courage to move forward. Valerie believed in Dorina when Dorina did not believe in herself.

Respect acknowledges healthy boundaries. Valerie set boundaries of time and resources by agreeing to spend three hours a week for one month with Dorina. Valerie shared resources that helped her get out of debt by establishing and maintaining a weekly budget. Valerie invited Dorina to a weekly Bible study, but respected Dorina's decision not to attend. Valerie respected Dorina's emotional boundary of grieving her husband's death at times and places of her choosing.

In summary, women in pain need to know

- I am not alone—*Listen to my story.*
- My feelings matter—*Empathize with me.*
- There is hope—*Reflect my options.*
- I can move forward—*Respect my choices.*

"Hurting people desperately want to be heard, understood, and invited to know God in the midst of their confusion."[6] A godly shepherd will draw women in pain to the very heart of God in the middle of their confusing pain through respectful listening, empathy, and reflection.

aspects of shepherding

As a sheep is dependent upon a shepherd to provide a healthy diet and climate for maximum growth, a shepherd is dependent upon the sheep to provide wool. In shepherding women, both the woman in pain and the shepherd play a critical role in providing a healthy outcome. As a shepherd cannot grow genuine wool, so a sheep cannot provide a healthy diet and climate for herself. Neither can a woman in emotional pain provide the healthy diet and climate she needs or the shepherd produce the needed outcomes for the woman.

As sheep and shepherd work together, so God intended members of His body to work in tandem. There are three aspects of shepherding that must work together simultaneously to bring healing:

1. What a shepherd can do
2. What a woman in pain can do
3. What a group can do

Almanda was afraid something awful would happen to her new baby daughter, Precious. Almanda was afraid God would punish her by taking Precious. Although Almanda did not recognize her over-possessive tendencies with her new baby daughter, Gloria did. Gloria extended friendship to Almanda and Precious. Soon Almanda talked to Gloria about her fears and eventually acknowledged her past abortion.

Gloria was able to bring what a shepherd can bring: active listening and empathy. Gloria's understanding of post-abortion stress enabled her to assess Almanda's fear of God's punishment and repeated nightmares. Almanda's deep depression and repeated illnesses on the anniversary date of the abortion further confirmed the source of her anxiety. Gloria's expressions of love and acceptance gave Almanda the strength she needed to acknowledge the source of her pain.

Gloria continued praying and giving appropriate biblical encouragement. But Gloria knew a group would be the best environment for Almanda to process the painful grief of her abortion and recommended this to Almanda. Almanda agreed to meet with a pregnancy resource center H.E.A.R.T. (Healing and Encouragement for Abortion Related Trauma) group for a fourteen-week study on abortion recovery.

Almanda soon learned that there were things only she could do in the healing process. She had to make a decision to attend the group each week. She had to take responsibility for her own grief work. She had to be willing to revisit her abortion within the protection of a safe and supportive group of women with similar stories. She had to give the group leader permission to gently lead her through the healing process each week. She had to choose to open her life to group members and to Gloria who faithfully walked alongside her during the fourteen weeks. She had to be willing to talk and listen in God's presence, to read His Word, ask His forgiveness, and receive His loving grace.

Almanda soon learned that a group encourages and supports you as you share your pain. The group message told her she was not alone. The women in the group understood and expressed care. They seemed to rally around each other, not interpreting or judging. The group's focus was on the power of Christ and the Bible to bring healing. Almanda drew strength from watching Christ's healing power work in each woman in her group. The group brought perspective and affirmation to Almanda's story.

It takes a community—the godly guidance of a shepherd, the personal work of the woman in pain, and the support of others who understand—to bring emotional healing. The interdependence of God's body working in tandem is a beautiful organism. It is, after all, God's plan for His children!

The strength of Christ's body is best seen in a team of shepherds, each member doing her part toward the ultimate goal of restoration. "Healing isn't something that happens *to* us through the people to whom we delegate that responsibility. Healing only happens *in* us as we ourselves walk through the pain and toward the hope that is held out before us."[7]

As Almanda took responsibility for her critical role and was willing to work in a healing community, her deep wound was cleansed and healed. Although a scar may always be there, Almanda is able to replace fear and depression with peace and contentment. And so it will be with other women who are carefully guided by shepherds of women.

a new model for shepherding women

OUR CHURCH *took* a survey of its women. It was an unusual survey—a long list of emotionally painful issues, with two columns to check: "I have in the past or am currently experiencing" and/or "I desire more information and resources." (See appendix A, "Grace Community Church Pastoral Care to Women Survey.") The responses surprised many. The large number of painful issues the majority of our women either presently experienced or encountered in the past was very great.

The women's ministry team discussed why those needs were so prevalent and why that so surprised them. Did the team need to establish a safe climate for sharing pain? Did team members need to be more authentic about their own painful issues? Would open discussions of painful issues send a message of acceptance and grace? The team's awareness had been raised. In the process, many on the team expressed a need to gain greater understanding of the issues causing our women pain.

DISCERN the NEED

Once the team consolidated the responses, it focused on the top five issues. After prayerful discussion, the team decided to address those issues during the coming year and work to provide ongoing support for women in pain.

The team informed the church as a whole of the needs and held Saturday Seminars on such topics as "Understanding the Pain of Divorce" to address them. Women in our body who had experienced divorce were personally invited. An open invitation was extended to others who wanted to understand and help women going through divorce. Our main speaker was from another church. After healing from the emotional pain of her divorce, she wrote a book on the topic and developed a ministry to both divorcées and caregivers.

The seminar facilitator, a divorcée herself, was strategically chosen from our church. She led those in attendance in follow-up discussion the second hour. She set the tone for acceptance and safety. She communicated understanding and grace to all, but particularly to those who had experienced divorce. She invited those attending to form a small support group.

This environment opened the door for women to share their hurts in our church. A similar format of addressing painful issues was repeated at several Saturday Seminars during that year.

BUILD the team

One of the primary purposes of our team was to provide ongoing support for women in pain. Although the women's ministry program in our church was flourishing, it was at a redefining juncture. Because building a new team takes time, it took us over a year to move through the small group stages of "forming, storming, and norming" before we could move to the stage of "performing." God put together a wonderful team of women who were willing to risk rebuilding, with its many unknowns.

During that first year, team members were willing to look at each member's gifts and season of life and the overall team profile. They discovered how one member's strength would cover another member's weakness. During that time nearly every member experienced emotional pain of some sort. Team members expressed support and care. Weekend retreats, Bible studies, and prayer drew the team together.

What is a team?

A team is a group of people with complementary skills who intentionally connect and collaborate for the purpose of accomplishing a mutually agreed upon goal.

My definition of team identifies *intentionality* as a critical component. Team members must be intentional about connecting and collaborating. Time spent "building history" together is time well spent. The people you trust the most are the people who have been in your life long enough to prove themselves trustworthy in a variety of situations. There is no microwave version of this essential ingredient. Team members *must* spend time together! This requires planning and implementation. Discovering complementary skills is a key part of that process.

The stronger the team, the greater the team's impact. Invest time in this early stage of developing effective ministry to women. Remember that the genetic relational fiber of a woman's being drives her to establish a relational bond before committing to a mutually agreed upon goal. So if a bond is established before the outward ministry begins, the team's impact will be greater and each team member will experience the joy of giving and receiving understanding and care from another. Soon you will hear, "Other women need to experience what we have on this team! What can we do to multiply our experience?"

Admittedly there are challenges inherent in team building, particularly if it is a new experience for team members. Women who have never had a positive team experience may be hesitant to enter one. Women will need to understand how important it is for them to contribute to the team process. Their contribution is critical on several levels.

- *Team members must be present at team gatherings.* This is essential. Since community and culture are both built when the team convenes, it is critical that each member be present to contribute to the process.
- *Team members must be willing to build history together.* This means participating together in new experiences. Team leaders should find ways for the team to jointly experience fun and adventure. Often the challenges along the way (a flat tire, illness, or bad weather) can be the most memorable. The way team members respond to these challenges is good training for meeting the challenges of ministry. Often teams will intentionally choose stretching experiences—such as taking a difficult course together or trying to reach the top of a rock climbing wall—to build cohesion and trust among their members.
- *Team members must be honest, transparent, and even vulnerable for maximum team development.* This requires a safe environment of acceptance, respect, and care. The team leader sets the pace and is key in maintaining the boundaries of respect and safety for all team members. This will involve building trust, which requires time and building history together.
- *Team members must foster a team spirit as opposed to a lone ranger mentality.* They must trade personal preferences and agendas for those of the team. Their ability to give for the benefit of the group must supersede giving for personal benefit. This will occur as team members grow in their ability to see the benefit of "team" versus "doing it myself."

It is hard for new members to bond with the established team members when the members are identified as "old" or "new." The new members can feel excluded as established members continually share past experiences: "How we did it last year." Since the team dynamics are changed with the addition of even one member, the team is in essence a new team when someone new joins. So the team will benefit when the team leader actually speaks of the entire team as "new" when someone joins or leaves. Redefining foundational elements and relationships enhances inclusion. Team members need to be given time to share their stories with the other members when a new team is formed. A team leader will find creative ways to deepen relationships through this sharing.

A team can accomplish together what no person could accomplish alone and have fun in the process! Nearly everyone wants to feel that he is a part of something bigger. Teams are the best way I know to have these advantages in ministry.

cast the VISION

As our team grew stronger, we cast a new vision. We challenged ourselves to find characteristics of poor shepherding and then the good shepherding spoken of, respectively, in Ezekiel 34 and John 10. We were open to modifying the traditional model of women's ministry to find the pattern given in Ezekiel 34. We identified four aspects of healthy ministry to women:

1. Feed the healthy
2. Strengthen the young
3. Care for the lost
4. Heal (or bind up) the injured

Our focus became "people groups." How would we provide food for healthy believers in Christ? How would we strengthen the young, care for the lost, and bind up the injured women in our church and community? As we continued to focus on these people groups, we realized that most women's ministry programs do well with the healthy. Some reach the young moms, and a few reach the lost. But seldom do ministries to women actually reach the injured. Perhaps that is why the voices of women in emotional pain often go unheard and effective care for them is rare.

We began to imagine a church that was more balanced in its approach to meeting the needs of women. We changed our nomenclature to reflect our focus. Our "Women's Ministry Program" was renamed "Pastoral Care to Women." We wanted to convey the idea that we cared about the whole person. No matter how many events or programs we had, underlying it all would be our purpose to give pastoral care, to shepherd our women.

The healthy, the young, the lost, and the injured sheep—our purpose was to minister to women in all of those places. We understood that all of us were or would be in one of those four spots during our lifetime. We desired to minister to each woman in such a way that she became a healthy reproducing shepherd.

We re-evaluated our current ministries on the basis of these questions:

1. For which primary target group (healthy, young, lost, injured) is this ministry designed?
2. What need is this program or study designed to meet?
3. Is this still a need in our body?
4. If so, how effective is this program in meeting this need?
5. If it is not effective, should we continue this program next year?
6. If it is effective, how can we make it even more effective next year?

We recognized that some ministries, such as a women's retreat, might change focus from year to year, thereby changing the primary target group. We also recognized that some ministries ministered to several target groups. Our challenge was to identify a primary group. Our planning became more strategic. We defined our goals more clearly, resulting in better outcomes.

After "Branch Shepherds" and "Branch Administrators" were identified for each of the four branches, the branches began to brainstorm on how to more effectively reach their target group. Each branch revisited existing ministries and began to develop new ones.

mold the ministry

We had assessed the needs of our women through the survey. Further prayer and discussion had enabled us to more clearly discern the needs. We had identified specific emotional needs we would address the next year. Now we needed to mold our ministry around those needs. The "Heal the Injured Branch" continued working on how to provide ongoing support for women in pain. A new ministry, "Shepherds of Women," developed. Some women were identified as shepherds of women. They shared these characteristics:

1. They had experienced emotional pain.
2. They had been restored to emotional health.
3. They were willing to help someone else experiencing similar pain.
4. They had received "Shepherds of Women" Training I and II.
5. They had received pastoral staff affirmation, which included confirmation that they fulfilled the four characteristics of the woman in Titus 2:3.
   a. They were "worthy of respect."
   b. They were "not slanderers."
   c. They had no known addictions.
   d. They were "able to teach" one-to-one what is biblically defined as good, sound in faith, love, and endurance.

It was made clear that to be identified as a shepherd of women did not mean that this woman was perfect or healthy in *every* area of her life (none would qualify if that were the standard). But it did mean that in the areas of experience in which she desired to minister, she was healthy and godly. Women were asked to complete a "Shepherd of Women Information Form" that identified the areas in which they were willing to minister to others. (See appendix B, "Shepherd of Women Information Form.")

Established training was repeated twice the first year. This basic training would be repeated as the need arose. The training included many of the elements of this book: the biblical basis for shepherding, compassion, and biblical examples of how Jesus treated women in pain. Women were given the opportunity to practice listening skills. Role-plays helped women see which words comforted and which ones hurt. The grief wheel was explained. Women learned that grief and loss are common experiences of women in pain and common also to many issues causing emotional pain. (See appendix D, "Grief and Loss Recovery.")

Recognized shepherds agreed to meet together three times a year for further consultation and training. Recommended resources, books, and videos were made available to the women. One resource was identified for discussion at most quarterly meetings. Each shepherd was "connected" to a shepherd on the Shepherds of Women Ministry Team for ongoing (monthly) communication. This limited meeting times yet kept the women in vital union with one another. It also gave the women a dependable resource and prayer partner in their shepherding roles.

Shepherds of women are available to pastoral staff and others in the church as needed. Requests for shepherding are submitted to the Shepherds of Women Ministry Coordinator. She gives the request to the shepherd best suited to the requested need. Confidentiality agreements prevent the shepherd from discussing details of her encounter without permission of the woman in pain. But her counterpart on the Shepherds of Women Ministry Team is informed of the meeting so that she can increase prayer for this shepherd as she meets with a woman in pain.

Often the question is raised about women not identified as shepherds who in fact shepherd other women. Are we leaving them out? No. The situation is parallel to a swimming team. Not every woman who enjoys swimming and is a good swimmer will be on a swimming team because of the greater commitment of time and energy that a team requires. Those who are on swimming teams generally expend the required time and energy for only a single season but may continue to spontaneously enjoy swimming throughout their lives.

Although women will shepherd other women naturally in the body (We encourage this!), the time commitment required to meet with other women and to engage in our quarterly meetings may not be possible in a given season of life. We encourage women to attend open seminars to gain more understanding, and we encourage them to minister to other women as God opens doors.

Younger women are especially encouraged to look at the possibility of developing as a shepherd of women. Biological age is not a factor in becoming a shepherd of women. Spiritual, mental, and emotional maturity are considered. Some of our best shepherds are young women. This is a wonderful way to "pass the baton" of ministry!

Shepherding also gives women an area of ministry to explore as they pursue their own gift development and church role. Bible study teachers and leaders and women's ministry directors are more visible role models. Ministry roles for women with strong mercy, encouragement, exhortation, discernment, and wisdom gifting may be harder to find. Women who are better listeners than speakers wonder if there is a place to serve. Although shepherds may reflect a wide variety of gifting and personalities, some are more naturally suited to the role. Role models for these women should be more visible.

Although this model is still developing, it is a beginning. If this model resonates with your heart's desire to minister to women, then may I suggest that you invite the women in your church who share that desire to join you in prayer. Rather than working to make an exact duplicate of the model in this chapter, ask God to make clear how

He wants you to provide effective shepherding in your particular culture and community. As you read this book together and pray, ask God to show you the next step.

Grace Bible Fellowship in Tangent, Oregon, did not have a formal group of "shepherds of women." Yet the essence of shepherding in the body of Christ was certainly modeled well in the story of Kenine and Cliff Stein. As new believers, Kenine and Cliff were eager to grow in their faith. Through a set of unpredictable circumstances, they found themselves in a closed cult-like situation that led to the death of their child and subsequent years in prison. Kenine was released before Cliff and began the journey of trying to make sense out of the faint imprint of her life that remained. Kenine had lost everything. The life of her younger son was gone, and the relationship with her remaining son appeared to be lost. She did not know if she would have a marriage when Cliff was released, nor if she would be able to rebuild one. She was stripped of her profession, the support of family, and her health. Few women would know the depth of her pain and emptiness. And where was God in all of this? Her best intentions—to follow Him—ended in disaster. Could she ever rebuild a meaningful life?

Don and Carol Bayne set the pace and many in their church followed. They simply were Jesus' hands and feet to Kenine. Ina Falk said, "God just told me to love you," and she spent the rest of her days doing so. Each Sunday, Ina, along with many other women in that church, hugged Kenine and whispered words of encouragement. Kenine's need for housing, transportation, employment, food, and even oil for her furnace were met by shepherds in this grace-filled church.

Immediate gratification was not the motive. It took time, and lots of it. Professional counseling, Bible studies, prayer groups, and many one-to-one conversations contributed to rebuilding Kenine's life. Women cried with her and walked beside her during those early years of pain. Together with Kenine they felt one major disappointment after another. They wisely knew when to take the initiative and when to wait for Kenine to take the initiative. "They were there for me. They loved me back to health," Kenine remembers. They shared both her tears and her joys.

Kenine recalls two additional keys to her recovery. One was allowing her the opportunity to minister to others in the midst of her own restoration. This communicated a powerful message of value, trust, and acceptance. Encouraging Kenine to utilize her gifts and abilities for the welfare of the body gave her hope for future usefulness.

The second key to recovery for Kenine was the opportunity to publicly share her heart and seek forgiveness for the reproach she felt she had inadvertently caused to the body of Christ. She needed to receive the love, grace, and forgiveness of the body of Christ.

Today, Kenine and Cliff have re-established their marriage and their home. They have been involved in ministry and training for further ministry effectiveness. Kenine knows firsthand what a shepherd to women looks like. She has seen many close-up. Kenine is one of the most effective shepherds I know. She is Jesus "with skin on" to every woman with whom she interfaces in a given day. She intentionally walks alongside women who are in seemingly hopeless situations. Kenine assures them, as only one who has walked her path can, that God will provide a way even when there seems to be no way.[1]

Are you be willing to be part of God's provision in the life of a woman like Kenine by shepherding a woman's heart?

appendix a

grace community church pastoral care to women survey

this confidential survey is designed to allow our women to give valuable input for future planning. Please complete the following questions and return to an usher at the end of the service or to the Pastoral Care to Women box in the foyer.

GENERAL INFORMATION

1. Which activities sponsored by GCC Pastoral Care to Women have you participated in this year?

Bible Study A.M. ____ P.M. ____   Retreat ____
Mary & Martha Live ____   Indoor Play Park _____
Christmas Dessert ____   Fall Kick-Off ____
Book Club ____   Valentine's Banquet ____
Beth Moore Day ____   Weigh Down ____
Aerobics ____   Spring Garden Luncheon ____

2. Age ____

3. Marital Status: Single ____ Married ____ Divorced ____
               Separated ____ Widowed ____

4. Primary Work/Career Focus:
   Full-time at home ____ Full-time outside the home ____
   Part-time in home ____
   Part-time outside home____Student____
   Occupation (optional) _____

5. Age(s) of children: _____

PASTORAL CARE INFORMATION

How would you describe your relationship with God at this point in your life?

   ____ Strong—I feel very close to God right now.
   ____ OK—I am following Him and seeking Him, but feel vulnerable at times
   ____ Weak—I am away from Him, distracted and caught up in my own world.

Please help us understand your needs by checking the appropriate boxes

	I have in the past or am currently experiencing	Desire more information and resources either for myself or someone I care about

Grief and Loss

Infertility	❑	❑
Miscarriage	❑	❑
Abortion	❑	❑
Widowhood	❑	❑
Divorce	❑	❑
Infidelity	❑	❑
Death of child	❑	❑
Other _____	❑	❑

Personal

Loneliness	❑	❑
Depression	❑	❑
Stress and/or anxiety	❑	❑
Homosexuality	❑	❑
Chronic illness or pain	❑	❑
Eating disorder(s)	❑	❑
Problems with alcohol or drugs (Rx or illicit)	❑	❑
Suicidal attempts or tendencies	❑	❑
Pornography	❑	❑
Postpartum blues/depression	❑	❑
Menopausal issues	❑	❑
Panic attacks	❑	❑
Depression	❑	❑
Post traumatic stress disorder	❑	❑
Other_____	❑	❑

	I have in the past or am currently experiencing	Desire more information and resources either for myself or someone I care about

Family

Single parent	❏	❏
Blended family	❏	❏
Unhappy marriage	❏	❏
Remarriage	❏	❏
Disabled family member	❏	❏
Chronic illness	❏	❏
Rebellion	❏	❏
Alcohol and/or drug issues	❏	❏
Care for elderly parent	❏	❏
Financial crises	❏	❏
Struggles with motherhood	❏	❏
Struggles with wife role	❏	❏
Husband who does not share faith	❏	❏
Emotionally challenged child(ren)	❏	❏
Physically challenged child(ren)	❏	❏
Other_____	❏	❏

Would you be willing to help other women in similar life experiences to your own? _____

In what areas specifically? _____

Are you interested in receiving training in these areas? _____

Please indicate in the comment section below (and on back) anything else you would like to mention. This is a good place to give us your input on what you would like to see developed in the area of pastoral care to women.

Comments:

If yes, or requesting more information on an issue, please include your name, e-mail, and phone number. Or contact us separate from this form.

Name (optional): _____

Phone (optional): _____ e-mail _____

Grace Community Church Pastoral Care to Women
SHEPHERD of WOMEN INFORMATION FORM

Name _____

Address _____ City _____

ZIP _____ E-mail_____ Phone (____)_____

A Shepherd of Women is someone who is willing to draw from her own relationship with Jesus Christ, life experience, gifts, and abilities to encourage another woman. Although a Shepherd of Women is still growing and learning, she is willing to give out of what she has gained in life to help another woman along the way. Her ultimate aim is to see the women she shepherds reach into Jesus' hand with a stronger "hold" than before.

Please check those areas in which you are willing to help others.

1. **Feed the healthy**

   I am willing to help a woman growing in her walk with God
   ____ Improve her prayer life
   ____ Enhance her quiet time with the Lord
   ____ Strengthen her spiritual disciplines (silence, prayer, meditation on the Bible, etc.)
   ____ Memorize Scripture
   ____ Study the Bible or a biblical topic
   ____ In this area _____

   _____

2. **Strengthen/seek the young**

   I am willing to help a younger woman
   ____ By discipling a new believer in Christ
   ____ Study a book of the Bible or biblical topic
   ____ In this practical way (e.g., role of wife, mom, homemaker, career, etc.) **Please be specific**

   _____

   _____

3. **Search/care for the lost**

   I am willing to help a non-Christian woman
   ____ By befriending her
   ____ By sharing the gospel with her
   ____ In this practical way

   _____

   _____

4. **Bind/heal the injured**

   I have a desire to come alongside other women who are going through emotionally painful situations. My own painful experiences have given me a compassion and desire to help women going through similar situations. I know the Chief Shepherd, my

Lord Jesus Christ, is the ONLY one who can truly bring soul healing. I understand I won't always have "answers," but I am willing to give understanding, acceptance, and support. I will obtain referral resources to offer when needed.

<u>Please check ONLY those experiences that you have personally had (or felt the impact as part of a family/friend who has experienced it) and received healing and ARE NOW WILLING TO HELP OTHERS IN SIMILAR SITUATIONS.</u>

"I've been there, I can help"

I am willing to help an "injured" woman who is faced with:

Grief & Loss
___ Infertility
___ Miscarriage
___ Abortion
___ Divorce
___ Infidelity
___ Broken home
___ Death of a young child
___ Death of an adult child
___ Death of a parent
___ Death of a sibling
___ Death of a spouse
___ Death of very close friend
___ Childhood sexual abuse
___ Loss of dreams or vision
___ Loss of job leading to extended unemployment
___ Other _____

Personal
___ Loneliness
___ Stress/Anxiety
___ Chronic illness or pain

___ Eating disorders
___ Problems with alcohol
___ Problems with drugs
___ Suicidal attempts or tendencies
___ Child abuse
___ Handicap _____
___ Addiction _____
___ Other _____

Family
___ Single parent
___ Blended family
___ Unhappy marriage/wife struggles
___ Unsaved husband
___ Infidelity
___ Pornography
___ Domestic violence
___ Verbal abuse
___ Emotional abuse
___ Remarriage
___ Disabled family member
___ Chronically ill family member
___ Emotionally challenged child(ren)
___ Prodigal child
___ Adopted child
___ Motherhood struggles
___ Alcoholic parent(s)
___ Drug use in family
___ Family financial crisis
___ Spouse's extended unemployment
___ Care for elderly family member
___ Other _____

I want to be identified as a Shepherd of Women at GCC.

1) This means I will be available for GCC pastors, church leaders, and pastoral care to women leaders to contact me with the names of women needing the kind of care I indicated on this form. I understand "available" means under normal circumstances I will be able to respond to their request, but have the freedom to decline if circumstances warrant.

2) This means I will participate in Shepherd of Women training at GCC.

Signature _____

Date _____

Thank you for allowing God to use your life experiences and abilities for the growth of the Body of Christ at Grace Community Church! Surely both you and the women you shepherd will be blessed as a result!

active Listening
exercises and
roLe pLays

1. Active Listening Exercises

For this exercise, divide your group into triads. Each triad should choose one of the following situations. After reading the situation, *individually* do the first two things. Have your triad work together on number three. Then share your answers with the whole group.

1. Underline the content (facts) of the message.

2. From the words listed under "Feeling Words and Possible Openers for Active Listening" (appendix E), choose ones you think describe what the speaker is feeling and write them down.

3. Write out a response that reflects what the speaker has just said. For example: It seems you are feeling _____ because _____.

SITUATION A. Since my husband has retired, he expects me to be at home all the time. He doesn't like my going to Bible study or working at the food shelter. I don't know what to do.

Underline the content (facts).

What do you think the speaker is feeling?

Write out a reflective response.

SITUATION B. One of my friends has turned her back on me. We have been friends for a long time, but when I see her, she won't speak to me.

Underline the content (facts).

What do you think the speaker is feeling?

Write out a reflective response.

SITUATION C. I can hardly wait! My husband and I are going to Florida next week and we have not been away for over two years.

Underline the content (facts).

What do you think the speaker is feeling? (Note that we share people's joy as well as their sorrow.)

Write out a reflective response.

SITUATION D. My daughter is failing in school. When I talk about it with my husband, he seems to act as if it doesn't matter to him.

Underline the content (facts).

What do you think the speaker is feeling?

Write out a reflective response.

SITUATION E. I just learned that my mother has cancer. She lives hundreds of miles from me.

Underline the content (facts).

What do you think the speaker is feeling?

Write out a reflective response.

2. Active Listening Role Play

a. For this exercise, divide your group into triads. Each triad should respond to this scenario in writing.

You meet Mary in the hallway at church and she tells you: "I love my job, but since Jamie was born, I can't seem to keep up. I don't like taking her to child care, but Tim says we need my income to stay in our new home."

Consider how you would respond to Mary, remembering the following:

1. Listen to Mary's feelings
2. Keep the focus on what Mary is saying, not on your need to fix her
3. Do not give advice or be judgmental

b. Find two volunteers to role-play this response:

Mary: "I love my job, but since Jamie was born, I can't seem to keep up. I don't like taking her to child care, but Tim says we need my income to stay in our new home."

You: "You seem to be feeling torn between working and staying at home."

Mary: "Yes, every morning when I leave for work there are dirty dishes in the sink and laundry to be done. Those are the first things I see when I get home."

You: "You're really struggling with all you have to do."

Mary: "That's right, and I don't think Tim understands how hard this schedule is for me. I really want to be with Jamie more."

You: "You feel Tim doesn't understand what it is like to be a mother and work at the same time."

Mary: "If he would just help me with dinner and bedtime, I could get caught up and spend more time with Jamie."

You: "Sounds like you may need to talk with Tim."

Mary: "That's right. I've been struggling with this on my own. Thanks for helping me see that I need to talk to Tim. I know he will help me."

c. Discuss

    1. How did Mary arrive at the conclusion that she needs to talk to Tim?

    2. Is her problem solved? Why or why not?

    3. How do you think active listening made her feel?

Carol Travilla, *Caring Without Wearing* (self-published by Carol Travilla, 4143 W. Bart Drive, Chandler AZ 85226, 1994), 32–37. Used by permission of the author.

grief and loss recovery

introductory discussion starters

A. Questions:
Use the following questions to begin discussion on experienced loss:

1. What do you remember about your first major loss? How old were you?
2. What feelings did you have?
3. Were you able to talk about it? With whom?
4. Did anyone try to explain the loss to you? Was he/she helpful?
5. What do you wish you would have understood then that you understand now about loss/grief?

B. Readings:

Use these readings to bring out feelings of loss within your discussion group. Ask, "Can anyone relate to these feelings and thoughts?"

ALONE

Holidays which were so special
That were anticipated and carefully planned for
Have now become fragile times
When my aloneness threatens to overwhelm

Times now are different
The kids are grown and gone
Chasing their own dreams and ambitions
They call and write, but it's not the same and it's not their fault

I try to count my blessings
To realize how much I do have
But on holidays especially
I feel alone

Around me I see families, laughing and playing
Talking, enjoying one another
And I wish only to get past the day
To not feel sorry for myself

So I return home alone
To the silence of empty rooms

BROKEN DREAMS

I feel like a sour dishrag
Crumpled and misused
Stinking from the residue of yesterday's unfulfilled promises
Mildewed from neglect
Soaked in the murky darkness of confusion

Never rinsed out
Never uncrumpled
Left to the stench of broken dreams

REBIRTH

The silent tears of the heart fall
Sending ripples in the puddle at my feet
How long will these fountains of tears bubble up?
How long?
As long as I am soundless, silent, quiet
The silent tears will not stop.
As I see and speak the truth
Truth about my pain and hurt
The dam is broken
The floodwaters of feelings may engulf for a time
But then comes in the jerky steps of recovery
The quiet joy of rebirth.

Grief is not a problem to be cured.
It is simply a statement
That you have loved someone.

Barbara Baumgardner, *A Passage Through Grief*, Broadman & Holman, 1997.

HE CARES

My God cares for me
He enters into my pain and suffering
and is present with me
My God is with me
Even in the times when my turmoil is so great
that I do not feel His presence
He is there working, drawing me back
into the quiet confidence that He cares
and the knowledge that He always will

INSTRUCTION ON UNDERSTANDING
Grief and Loss

There are many good resources on grief and loss. Access them and choose those that work best for your particular needs. The following notes are brief, just to get you started. The handout on page 192 may be used for instructive purposes. Responses to handout questions are as follows:

I. The griever is at a crossroad where a decision must be made.[1]
  A. *Denial*
  B. *Withdrawal*

  Both of these responses say that God is not enough, not good enough, or not big enough. As Adam and Eve covered themselves with fig leaves, we too can disguise or cover our pain, vulnerability, and true neediness.

  C. *Acknowledgment:* I must acknowledge:

  1. *What loss means to me.* I will never be the same and neither will my world. I need to acknowledge what I have lost and how my life will be different.
  2. *My emotions.* I must feel the emotions. I may feel anguish, despair, anger, numbness, depression, or confusion. These are "normal" grieving emotions and feeling them is essential for healing.
  3. *That I have doubts at many levels.* I may question what I have believed about God and life. I need to bring these questions out into the open. God is big enough to handle rage and doubts.

     When my brother died in a plane crash, an older man who had earlier lost his adult son spoke at the memorial service. With the passion of ongoing grief and determined hope, he looked into the eyes of our grieving family and said, "Don't be afraid to ask the hard questions. You may not find answers, but you will find God. God reveals Himself to people who have the courage to fully enter their confusion and heartache."[2]

4. *The mystery of God.* God's ways are inscrutable. God cannot be controlled. He is not under obligation to explain His ways to us. I need to embrace the mysterious ways of God.

II. What Jesus teaches us about grief from John 11
   A. The timing of Jesus' intervention in life's tragedies is *not an indicator of His love.*
   B. Jesus shares *our sorrows.*
   C. Our response in crisis will be either to step toward God or to *step away from God.*

GRIEF AND LOSS

I. The griever is at a crossroads where a decision must be made:
   A. Shall I return to life the way I knew it before my loss?

   _____

   B. Shall I create a world of fantasy where good always triumphs?

   _____

   C. Shall I face the reality of grief?

   _____

   1. I must confess _____
   2. I must accept and _____
   3. I must face the fact _____

> Don't be afraid to ask the hard questions. You may not find answers, but you will find God. God reveals Himself to people who have the courage to fully enter their confusion and heartache. (Larry Crabb Jr.)

   4. I need to embrace _____

II. What Jesus teaches us about grief from John 11
   A. The timing of Jesus' intervention in life's tragedies is

   _____
   (John 11:3, 5-6)
   B. Jesus shares _____
   (John 11:33-35)
   C. Our response in crisis will be either _____
   Or _____
   (John 11:45-47)

LOSS-RECOVERY WHEEL

There are many versions of the grief process. The Loss-Recovery Wheel[3] depicts the recurring feelings and repetitive nature of grief (see following page).

1. First Stage: PROTEST
   TASK: Accept the reality of the loss.
   Words I may hear myself say: *Nothing is wrong; nothing has really happened.*

2. Second Stage: DESPAIR
   TASK: Experience the pain of grief.
   Words I may hear myself say: *I know I can't make it; I'm not sure I'm going to survive.*

3. Third Stage: DETACHMENT
   TASK: Adjust to an environment in which the loss exists.
   Words I may hear myself say; *I am not interested; it won't be the same.*

4. Fourth Stage: RECOVERY
   TASK: Withdraw emotional energy from the old and reinvest it in the new.
   Words I may hear myself say: *I haven't done this before; it is actually enjoyable.*

Our best contribution to the one who grieves may be our presence and our box of tissues. An anonymous story says it best.

> Her little girl was late arriving home from school, so the mother began to scold her:
> "Why are you so late?"
> "I had to help another girl. She was in trouble."
> "What did you do to help her?"
> "Oh, I sat down and helped her cry."

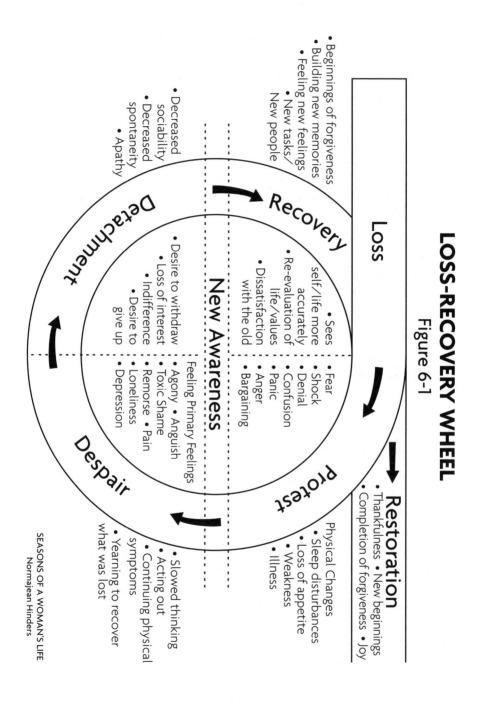

LOSS-RECOVERY WHEEL
Figure 6-1

Loss

Recovery

• Sees self/life more accurately
• Re-evaluation of life/values
• Dissatisfaction with the old

Detachment

• Decreased sociability
• Decreased spontaneity
• Apathy

• Beginnings of forgiveness
• Building new memories
• Feeling new feelings
• New tasks/ New people

New Awareness

• Desire to withdraw
• Loss of interest
• Indifference
• Desire to give up

Despair

• Yearning to recover what was lost
• Slowed thinking
• Acting out
• Continuing physical symptoms

Feeling Primary Feelings
• Agony • Anguish
• Toxic Shame
• Remorse • Pain
• Loneliness
• Depression

• Fear
• Shock
• Denial
• Confusion
• Panic
• Anger
• Bargaining

Protest

Physical Changes
• Sleep disturbances
• Loss of appetite
• Weakness
• Illness

Restoration
• Thankfulness • New beginnings
• Completion of forgiveness • Joy

SEASONS OF A WOMAN'S LIFE
Normajean Hinders

a List of feeLING words

Abandoned	Committed	Disgusted
Accepted	Compassionate	Distant
Affectionate	Competent	Dominated
Afraid	Concerned	Doubtful
Alarmed	Confused	Embarrassed
Angry	Cowardly	Empty
Annoyed	Cruel	Envious
Anxious	Curious	Evasive
Appreciated	Defeated	Exhausted
Awkward	Dejected	Excited
Beaten	Dependent	Exhilarated
Bewildered	Depressed	Fearful
Bitter	Deprived	Frigid
Calm	Deserving	Frustrated
Closed	Desperate	Furious
Comfortable	Disappointed	Glad

Grieved
Guilty
Gutless
Happy
Helpless
Hopeful
Hopeless
Horrified
Hostile
Hurt
Hypercritical
Ignored
Immobilized
Impatient
Inadequate
Incompetent
Indecisive
Inferior
Insecure
Insincere
Irritated
Isolated
Jealous
Judgmental
Lonely
Lovable
Loyal
Manipulated

Melancholy
Misunderstood
Needy
Neglected
Nervous
Offended
Optimistic
Overlooked
Peaceful
Persecuted
Pessimistic
Phony
Pleased
Preoccupied
Pressured
Proud
Rejected
Remorseful
Repelled
Repulsive
Resentful
Revengeful
Sad
Scared
Shocked
Shy
Sincere
Sorry

Stupid
Suicidal
Supported
Suspicious
Sympathetic
Tense
Terrified
Threatened
Tired
Torn
Unappreciated
Uncertain
Undecided
Unresponsive
Uptight
Used
Useless
Vengeful
Victimized
Violent
Warm
Weak
Weary
Weepy
Wishy-washy
Withdrawn
Worn out
Youthful

notes

Chapter 2: The Need for Shepherds of Women

1. Brenda Hunter, *In the Company of Women* (Sisters, Ore.: Multnomah, 1994), 21, 23.

2. Archibald Hart, Gary Gulbranson, and Jim Smith, *Mastering Pastoral Counseling*, Mastering Ministry Series (Sisters, Ore.: Multnomah, 1992), 110–21.

3. M. Gay Hubbard, *Women: The Misunderstood Majority*, Contemporary Christian Counseling Series, No. 4, Gary R. Collins, gen. ed. (Nashville: Word, 1992), 5.

4. Jean Lush, *Emotional Phases of a Woman's Life* (Grand Rapids: Baker, 1998), 20.

5. Ibid., 51, followed by 44.

6. Ibid., 20.

7. Maxine Glaz and Jeanne Stevenson Moessner, ed., *Women in Travail and Transition* (Minneapolis: Fortress, 1991), 19.

8. Larry Crabb, *Men and Women* (Grand Rapids: Zondervan, 1991), 160.

9. Jeanne Stevenson Moessner, ed., *Through the Eyes of Women: Insights for Pastoral Care* (Minneapolis: Fortress, 1996), 20.

10. Ruth Senter, *Have We Really Come a Long Way?* (Minneapolis: Bethany, 1997), 23.

11. William McRae, *The Dynamics of Spiritual Gifts* (Grand Rapids: Zondervan, 1980), 86

12. I am indebted to Kay Bruce, Psy.D., Associate Professor of Counseling, Western Seminary, Portland, Oregon, and Executive Director, Charis Counseling Associates, Vancouver, Washington, 1997–present, for many of the insights that appear in this list of components.

Chapter 3: Eternal Understanding: Biblical Basis

1. See John Coe, "Being Faithful to Christ in One's Gender: Theological Reflections on Masculinity and Femininity," in *Women and Men in Ministry: A Complementary Perspective*, ed. Robert L. Saucy and Judith K. TenElshof (Chicago: Moody, 2001), 193, for a fuller discussion of Adam's being completed in Eve.

2. John H. Sailhamer, *Genesis*, vol. 2, *The Expositor's Bible Commentary*, ed. Frank E. Gaebelein (Grand Rapids: Zondervan, 1990), 58.

3. I am indebted to Jan Verbruggen, Ph. D., Associate Professor of Old Testament Language and Literature, Western Seminary, and James DeYoung, Th.D., Professor of New Testament Language and Literature, Western Seminary, for many of the concepts developed in this discussion.

Chapter 4: Internal Understanding: Essence of Womanhood

1. Anne Moir and David Jessel, *Brain Sex* (New York: Bantam Doubleday, 1989), 36.

2. Melinda Dodd and Kalia Doner, "The Get-Smart Health Guide," *Working Mother*, February 2002, 52–53. See also an Internet article, "Male-Female Differences," at www.brainplace.com.

3. Bill Farrel and Pam Farrel, *Men Are Like Waffles, Women Are Like Spaghetti* (Eugene, Ore.: Harvest House, 2001), 13.

4. Moir and Jessel, *Brain Sex*, 100.

5. Ibid., 48.

6. Ibid., 101, 137.

7. Deborah Blum, *Sex on the Brain* (New York: Penguin, 1997), xxi.

8. Jean Lush, *Emotional Phases of a Woman's Life* (Grand Rapids: Revell, 1987), 20.

9. Ibid., 50.

10. Dr. Barbara Sherwin, interviewed by Gail Sheehy, November 1994, reported in Gail Sheehey, *New Passages: Mapping Your Life Across Time* (New York: Ballantine, 1995), 220. See also Barbara Sherwin and Diane L. Kampen, "Estrogen Use and Verbal Memory in Healthy Postmenopausal Women," *Obstetrics and Gynecology* 83, no. 6 (June 1994), 979–83.

11. Sheehy, *New Passages*, 217–18.

12. Margaret Gorman, "Midlife Transitions in Men and Women," in Robert J. Wicks, Richard D. Parsons, Donald Capps, and M. Scott Peck, eds., *Clinical Handbook of Pastoral Counseling*, expanded edition, Integration Books (New York: Paulist, 1993), 306.

13. Ibid., 298.

14. Daniel Levinson, *The Seasons of a Woman's Life* (New York: Knopf, 1996), 21.

15. Charles M. Sell, *Transitions Through Adult Life* (Grand Rapids: Zondervan, 1991); also Gail Sheehy, *New Passages*.

16. David Olson, *Families: What Makes Them Work* (Beverly Hills, Calif.: Sage, 1983).

17. Ibid.

18. Sheehy, *New Passages*, 5.

19. Ibid.

20. Ibid., 320.

21. Ibid., 327.

22. Ibid., 327.

23. Adam Bryant and Erika Check, "How Parents Raise Boys and Girls," *Newsweek Special Issue* (Fall/Winter 2000), 64–65.

24. M. Gay Hubbard, *Women: The Misunderstood Majority*, Contemporary Christian Counseling, Gary R. Collins, gen. ed. (Nashville: Word, 1992), 1, 5.

25. Ibid., 6–7.

26. Lawrence Kohlberg, *The Psychology of Moral Development: The Nature and Validity of Moral Stages*, Essays on Moral Development, vol. 2 (San Francisco: Harper & Row, 1984).

27. Hubbard, *Women*, 149.

28. Ibid., 40.

29. Mary K. Kassian, *The Feminist Gospel* (Wheaton, Ill.: Crossway, 1992).

30. *Webster's Encyclopedic Unabridged Dictionary of the English Language* (New York: Random, 1996), 1561.

31. Jim Smith, "Counseling Men, Counseling Women," in Archibald D. Hart, Gary L. Gulbranson, and Jim Smith, eds., *Mastering Pastoral Counseling* (Bend, Ore.: Multnomah Press and Christianity Today, Inc., 1992), 110–21.

32. Ibid., 111.

33. Jean Baker Miller, "The Development of Women's Sense of Self," *Work in Progress*, no. 12 (Wellesley, Mass.: Stone Center, 1984).

34. Nancy Chodorow, *The Reproduction of Mothering: Psychoanalysis and the Sociology of Gender* (Berkeley: Univ. of California Press, 1978).

35. Hubbard, *Women*, 55.

36. Jean Baker Miller, *Toward a New Psychology of Women* (Boston: Beacon, 1976), 83. [A second edition was issued 1986.]

37. Marilyn Loden, *Feminine Leadership: Or How to Succeed in Business Without Being One of the Boys* (New York: Random House, 1985), 134–35.

38. James Dobson, *Bringing Up Boys* (Wheaton, Ill.: Tyndale, 2001), 19, 20.

39. "Day Care on Job," Working, Section G, *Orlando Sentinel*, 18 July 2001.

40. Norma Schweitzer Wood, "An Inquiry into Pastoral Counseling Ministry Done by Women in the Parish Setting," *The Journal of Pastoral Care* 50, no. 4 (Winter 1996), 345.

41. Smith, "Counseling Men, Counseling Women," 112.

42. Carol Gilligan, *In a Different Voice* (Cambridge, Mass.: Harvard Univ. Press, 1982).

43. Archibald D. Hart, Catherine Hart Weber, and Debra Taylor, *Secrets of Eve* (Nashville: Word, 1998), 45.

44. Smith, "Counseling Men, Counseling Women," 113.

45. Gilligan, *In a Different Voice*, 174.

46. Smith, "Counseling Men, Counseling Women," 112, 120.

47. "You May Have Always Suspected It, But a Study Suggests That Women *Do* Cope with

Stress Differently Than Men," 30 August 2000, www.psu.edu/ur/2000/womenstress. This is a key finding from a UCLA-led study, *Behavioral Response to Stress in Females: Tend-and-Befriend, Not Fight-or-Flight*, led by Dr. Shelley E. Taylor, Dr. Laura Klein of Penn State's College of Health and Human Development; Brian P. Lewis, Assistant Professor at Syracuse; Regan A. R. Gurung, Assistant Professor at the University of Wisconsin, Green Bay; and UCLA graduate students Tara L. Gruenewald and John A. Updegraff.

48. Ibid.

49. Mary Field Belenky, Blythe McVicker Clinchy, Nancy Rule Goldburger, and Jill Mattuck Tarule, *Women's Ways of Knowing: The Development of Self, Voice, and Mind* (New York: BasicBooks, HarperCollins, 1986).

50. Belenky et al., *Women's Ways of Knowing*, 180.

51. Deborah Tannen, *You Just Don't Understand* (New York: Ballantine, 1990).

52. Ibid.

53. Ibid.

54. Lillian Glass, *He Says, She Says* (New York: Putnam, 1992), 77–79.

55. Tannen, *You Just Don't Understand*.

Chapter 5: External Understanding: Backdrop of Pastoral Care to Women

1. "Day Care on Job," Section G, Working, *Orlando Sentinel*, 18 July 2001.

2. Patricia Aburdene and John Naisbitt, *Megatrends for Women* (New York: Villard, 1992).

3. Liz Nickles and Laurie Ashcraft, *Update: Woman*, Patricia Edmonds, "Now the Word Is Balance," *USA Weekend*, 23–25 October 1998; the data in this paragraph are taken from this and another article on the Web, some as direct quotation, some as paraphrase. These articles are best accessed through Google using the search request: USA Weekend: "What Women Want Now."

4. "Human Rights and Political Decision-Making," chapter 6 of *The World's Women 2000: Trends and Statistics* (New York: United Nations, 2000), 153.

5. S. G. Diniz et al., "Gender Violence and Reproductive Health," *International Journal of Obstetrics and Gynecology* 63, no. 1 (1998).

6. M. Crawford et al., "Women Killing: Intimate Femicide in Ontario 1974–1990," unpublished (1991).

7. J. Arbuckel et al., "Safe at Home? Domestic Violence and Other Homicides Among Women in New Mexico," *Annals of Emergency Medicine* 27, no. 2 (1997).

8. "Human Rights and Political Decision-Making," 153.

9. Dr. Elizabeth Negi, "Hard Choices or Soft Options?" *Dharma Deepika: A South Asian Journal of Missiological Research*, no. 1 (January–June 2001), 3–8.

10. "Human Rights and Political Decision-Making," 160.

11. Ibid., 160–61.

12. Ibid., 156, 161.

13. Ibid., 67.

14. Ibid., 68.

15. Ibid., 110.

16. Lorry Lutz, *Women of the 10/40 Window,* Women of Global Action Booklet, 9.

17. Miriam Adeney, *Daughters of Islam: Building Bridges with Muslim Women* (Downers Grove, Ill.: InterVarsity, 2002).

18. Karen Neumann, interview, 27 February 2002, Portland, Oregon.

19. "Women Are the Backbone of the Christian Congregations in America," *Barna Research Online,* www.barna.org, archive section for 6 March 2000. All quotations and statistics from Barna are taken from this article.

20. Ruth Senter, *Have We Really Come a Long Way?* (Minneapolis: Bethany House, 1997), 87–89.

Chapter 6: Compassion Comes from Understanding Like-Pain

1. *New American Standard Exhaustive Concordance of the Bible,* Robert L. Thomas, gen. ed. (Nashville: Holman Bible Publishers, 1981), 1682.

2. *Webster's Encyclopedic Unabridged Dictionary of the English Language* (N.Y.: Random House, 1996), 416.

3. *The Expositor's Bible Commentary,* Frank E. Gaebelein, gen. ed., vol 8 (Grand Rapids: Zondervan, 1984), 943.

4. *The NIV Study Bible,* Kenneth Barker, gen. ed. (Grand Rapids: Zondervan, 1995), 1558.

5. Ibid., 1598.

6. *Studies in the Four Gospels,* "The Gospel According to Luke," G. Campbell Morgan (Westwood, N.J.: Revell, 1931), 139.

7. Ann Petrie and Jeanette Petrie, with Richard Attenborough, *Mother Teresa* (Petrie Productions, 1986), video.

8. Helen Kooiman Hosier, *100 Christian Women Who Changed the 20th Century* (Grand Rapids: Revell, 2000), 285.

9. Ibid., 285–86.

10. Ibid., 287.

11. Ibid., 288, 284.

12. *Ladies Home Journal,* "100 Most Important Women of the 20th Century" (Des Moines, Iowa: Meredith Corporation, 1998), 53.

13. Frank E. Gaebelein, gen. ed., *The Expositor's Bible Commentary,* vol 8, *Matthew,* D. A. Carson (Grand Rapids: Zondervan Regency Reference Library, 1984), 235.

14. Ibid.

15. Phillip Keller, *A Shepherd Looks at Psalm 23* (Grand Rapids: Zondervan, 1970), 60–63.

16. Ibid., 63.

17. Story and moral freely adapted from www.sermonillustrator.org/illustrator/seattle.htm.

Chapter 7: The Master Shepherd Met Women at Their Point of Pain

1. *The New International Study Bible,* Kenneth Barker, gen. ed. (Grand Rapids: Zondervan, 1995), note at John 4:26 [page 1598].

2. Dr. W. David Hager, *As Jesus Cared for Women* (Grand Rapids: Baker, 1998), 182.

3. Thomas Boomershine, *Story Journey: An Invitation to the Gospel as Storytelling* (Nashville: Abingdon, 1988), 158.

4. Frederick Buechner, *Telling Secrets* (San Francisco: HarperSanFrancisco, 1991), 30.

5. Boomershine, *Story Journey*, 19.

Chapter 8: Profile of a Good Shepherd

1. Sandy and Greg Wellman's story is used by permission given to the author, May 2002.

2. From a lecture by Eddie Gibbs at Western Seminary, Portland, Oregon, 21 March 2002.

3. Phillip Keller, *A Shepherd Looks at the Good Shepherd and His Sheep* (Grand Rapids: Zondervan, 1978), 29.

4. Ibid., 40–41.

5. Alice Mathews, *A Woman God Can Lead* (Grand Rapids: Discovery House, 1998), 329.

Chapter 9: The Skill of Shepherding Women

1. Carol Travilla, *Caring Without Wearing* (self-published, Carol Travilla, 4143 W. Bart Drive, Chandler AZ 85226, 1994), 54.

2. *Webster's Encyclopedic Unabridged Dictionary of the English Language* (New York: Random House, 1996), 638.

3. Leslie Virgo, ed., "Skills of Pastoral Care," chap. 14, *First Aid in Pastoral Care* (Edinburgh: T. & T. Clark, 1987), 173.

4. Ibid., 174.

5. Catherine Clark Kroeger and James R. Beck, ed., *Women, Abuse, and the Bible* (Grand Rapids: Baker, 1996), 18.

6. Larry Crabb and Dan Allender, *Hope When You Are Hurting* (Grand Rapids: Zondervan, 1996), 84.

7. Marion Duckworth, *Healing for the Empty Heart* (Minneapolis: Bethany House, 1993), 59.

Chapter 10: A New Model for Shepherding Women

1. Kenine and Cliff Stein's story, which appears in chapter 10, is used by permission of the Steins granted to author on May 2002.

Appendix D: Grief and Loss Recovery

1. Resource for Section I is Liam Atchison and Precious Atchison, *Grief* (Colorado Springs: NavPress, 1993).

2. Larry Crabb Jr., *Grief*, Liam & Precious Atchison (Colorado Springs: NavPress, 1993), 6.

3. The "Loss Recovery Wheel," is taken from a book written by psychotherapist Normajean Hinders, *Seasons of a Woman's Life* (Nashville: Broadman & Holman, 1994), 68, which explores the psychological, emotional, and spiritual development of women. Used by permission.

SINCE 1894, Moody Publishers has been dedicated to equip and motivate people to advance the cause of Christ by publishing evangelical Christian literature and other media for all ages, around the world. Because we are a ministry of the Moody Bible Institute of Chicago, a portion of the proceeds from the sale of this book go to train the next generation of Christian leaders.

If we may serve you in any way in your spiritual journey toward understanding Christ and the Christian life, please contact us at www.moodypublishers.com.

"All Scripture is God-breathed and is useful for teaching, rebuking, correcting and training in righteousness, so that the man of God may be thoroughly equipped for every good work."
—2 TIMOTHY 3:16, 17

MOODY
PUBLISHERS

THE NAME YOU CAN TRUST®

WESTERN SEMINARY
WOMEN'S CENTER *for* *Ministry*

We prepare and involve women in ministry

For information on courses and events especially designed for women in leadership and ministry, check out our offerings at www.westernseminary.edu/women/ or contact us at wcm@ westernseminary.edu

Women's Center for Ministry
Western Seminary
5511 SE Hawthorne Blvd.
Portland, OR 97215
1-800-547-4546, ext. 1931
503-517-1931

Western Seminary offers the following graduate programs in pastoral care to women:

Master of Divinity open track in Pastoral Care to Women
Master of Arts Specialized in Pastoral Care to Women
Graduate Studies Diploma in Pastoral Care to Women

The Center for Life Long Learning at Western Seminary offers non-credit programs (no undergraduate degree required) such as:

Advanced Studies Certificate in Pastoral Care to Women

The vision of the Women's Center for Ministry at Western Seminary is to become a global hub of training, resources, and networking for women in ministry.

SHEPHERDING A WOMAN'S HEART TEAM

ACQUIRING EDITOR:
Elsa Mazon

COPY EDITOR:
Anne Scherich

BACK COVER COPY:
Julie-Allyson Ieron, Joy Media

COVER DESIGN:
Ragont Design

INTERIOR DESIGN AND ILLUSTRATIONS:
Ragont Design

PRINTING AND BINDING:
Versa Press Incorporated

The typeface for the text of this book is
Weiss